Strategies to Overcome Office Challenges

C. P. Kumar
Reiki Healer
Roorkee - 247667, India

Disclaimer

While every effort has been made to ensure the accuracy and completeness of the content in this book, the author cannot guarantee that the information contained herein is error-free, up-to-date, or suitable for every individual circumstance.

The author shall not be held liable or responsible for any errors or omissions in the content of the book, nor for any damages, or losses that may arise from any actions taken based upon the suggestions or contents presented in the book.

Readers are advised to use their own judgment and discretion in applying the information provided in this book, and to consult with qualified professionals before taking any action based on the contents of this book. The author disclaims any and all liability or responsibility for any actions taken or not taken based on the information contained in this book.

DEDICATION

To all those who have experienced the complexities of the modern workplace, this book is dedicated to you. Your resilience, determination, and unwavering commitment to overcoming office challenges have inspired the creation of this comprehensive guide. In your pursuit of success and well-being, you have demonstrated that every obstacle is an opportunity, and every challenge is a chance for growth.

May the strategies outlined in these pages serve as a source of knowledge and empowerment, helping you navigate the ever-evolving landscape of the office with confidence and grace. Your dedication and perseverance are a testament to the potential within each of us to triumph over adversity.

This book is dedicated to you, the champions of the office, who continuously strive to turn challenges into triumphs. Your pursuit of excellence fuels the progress of the modern workplace and sets a shining example for all who follow.

C. P. Kumar

CONTENTS

PREFACE

In a world defined by constant change, the modern office has become a dynamic battleground for both employers and employees. It is a place where challenges emerge, shift, and evolve in response to the ever-advancing technologies, diverse workforce dynamics, and the increasingly complex global economy. The office environment, once characterized by traditional structures and routines, has undergone a remarkable transformation. As we navigate this ever-shifting terrain, it is crucial to equip ourselves with the knowledge and strategies needed to overcome the myriad challenges we encounter on a daily basis.

This book, "Strategies to Overcome Office Challenges", serves as your compass in the labyrinth of modern office life. Within these pages, you will embark on a comprehensive journey to understand, confront, and conquer the diverse challenges that emerge in today's workplaces.

The evolution of office challenges is at the heart of this exploration, and the journey begins with a comprehensive understanding of the origins of these challenges. We'll delve into the roots of workplace adversity and examine how the traditional office setting has given way to a dynamic, ever-changing landscape.

The chapters that follow will address the multifaceted nature of the challenges we encounter. From technological disruptions that test our adaptability to interpersonal conflicts that affect our relationships, from the relentless pursuit of time management mastery to the insidious threats of stress and burnout, each chapter offers a toolkit of strategies to help you navigate and conquer specific challenges.

Moreover, this book takes a holistic approach to office life. We examine the physical and mental health implications, explore the art of self-management, scrutinize the pivotal role of leadership, and dissect common challenges across various office roles. Sales and marketing professionals, IT and technical support experts, managers and leaders, human resources specialists, and finance and accounting professionals will all find tailored insights to bolster their careers and well-being.

Communication and technology, pivotal components of the modern workplace, are given special attention, and we explore how innovation and change shape the future of office work. Legal issues and compliance are unraveled, offering clarity in a world marked by regulatory complexity.

As you traverse these pages, you'll find practical guidance to help you overcome the obstacles that stand in your way. This book is not just a resource; it is a companion for your journey through the challenges of the modern office.

At the end of your expedition, you will discover key takeaways that serve as your North Star, guiding your path toward a future marked by the adaptability and resilience required for success in the ever-evolving world of office work.

In a time when the workplace is evolving at an unprecedented pace, "Strategies to Overcome Office Challenges" is your roadmap for thriving amidst change, building meaningful relationships, and achieving your personal and professional goals. Welcome to a comprehensive guide that not only addresses the challenges of today but also prepares you for the office of tomorrow.

C. P. Kumar

Reiki Healer
Former Scientist 'G', National Institute of Hydrology
Roorkee - 247667, India
Web: https://www.angelfire.com/nh/cpkumar/virgo.html

The modern workplace is a dynamic and ever-evolving landscape, filled with a myriad of challenges that employees and organizations must navigate. From the rapid advancement of technology to the complexities of interpersonal relationships, the office environment is rife with obstacles waiting to be overcome. In this article, we will explore the introduction to office challenges, setting the stage for a comprehensive understanding of the issues that individuals and companies face in the contemporary business world.

Setting the Stage for Office Challenges

The office, whether physical or virtual, serves as the battleground for numerous challenges that can impact productivity, morale, and overall success. Setting the stage for these challenges is crucial to understanding their origins and finding effective strategies to overcome them.

The Changing Nature of Work: The way we work has transformed significantly in recent years. Remote work, flexible schedules, and the rise of the gig economy have all contributed to a shifting landscape where traditional office structures are no longer the norm.

Technological Disruptions: Technology, while offering unprecedented opportunities for efficiency, has introduced its own set of challenges. Cybersecurity threats, data breaches, and the relentless pace of software updates can disrupt even the most well-established work routines.

Interpersonal Dynamics: The workplace is a social ecosystem, and human interactions are fraught with the potential for conflict. Managing interpersonal conflicts, fostering effective communication, and building strong, harmonious teams are perpetual challenges.

Time Management: As the demands on our time and attention grow, mastering time management becomes increasingly crucial. Efficiently allocating time to tasks, projects, and personal well-being is a challenge that plagues many office workers.

Stress and Burnout: The modern office can be a breeding ground for stress and burnout, with heavy workloads, tight deadlines, and the constant need to stay connected. Recognizing the signs and addressing these issues is essential for maintaining a healthy work-life balance.

The Evolution of Office Challenges

To understand the challenges of the modern office fully, it's important to recognize how these issues have evolved over time. As the workplace has changed, so too have the challenges that accompany it.

From Typewriters to AI: The evolution of technology is perhaps the most significant driver of change in the workplace. From typewriters and filing cabinets to artificial intelligence and cloud computing, the tools and systems we use have transformed the way we work.

From Cubicles to Collaboration: The physical environment of the office has also undergone a transformation. The traditional cubicle, once synonymous with office life, has given way to open-plan offices, co-working spaces, and virtual workplaces that emphasize collaboration and flexibility.

From Supervision to Autonomy: The traditional top-down management model is evolving towards a more autonomous and self-directed approach. Employees are increasingly expected to take ownership of their work and contribute to decision-making processes.

From Local to Global: The global nature of business means that teams and partners can be spread across the world. This has introduced new challenges related to different time zones, cultural differences, and the need for effective virtual communication.

From Physical to Mental Health: Workplace challenges have expanded beyond physical well-being to encompass mental health issues. Recognizing the importance of mental health and providing support is a relatively recent but critical development.

Conclusion

In this article, we have explored the introduction to office challenges, setting the stage for a comprehensive understanding of the issues faced in the modern workplace. From the ever-changing nature of work to the challenges posed by technology, interpersonal dynamics, and time management, the office environment is replete with obstacles that require innovative strategies to overcome.

As we delve into the chapters of the book "Strategies to Overcome Office Challenges", we will explore these issues in greater depth and provide practical insights and solutions for individuals and organizations striving to thrive in the face of these challenges. By acknowledging the evolution of office challenges and embracing the opportunities for growth and improvement, we can pave the way for a more harmonious, productive, and sustainable future in the world of work.

Chapter 2. Embracing Technology
Strategies for Dealing with Technological Disruptions

Introduction

In today's fast-paced and technology-driven world, businesses and offices face constant challenges in adapting to and leveraging new technologies. The digital age has ushered in a multitude of innovations, from artificial intelligence and automation to cloud computing and the Internet of Things. While these advancements offer great potential, they also bring about technological disruptions that can be daunting for many. This article explores the strategies for dealing with technological disruptions, offering insights into how businesses and individuals can adapt to the ever-evolving tech landscape.

Technology, often seen as a double-edged sword, has revolutionized the way we work and conduct business. It has streamlined processes, improved efficiency, and created new opportunities. However, it has also introduced a set of challenges that can disrupt operations, stifle productivity, and cause anxiety in the workplace.

The rapid pace of technological advancement can be overwhelming, leaving many organizations and individuals struggling to keep up. In this article, we will address these common technology-related challenges and explore strategies to foster technological resilience.

Common Technology-Related Challenges

Rapid Technological Obsolescence: One of the primary challenges faced in the tech-savvy world is the rapid obsolescence of technology. What was cutting-edge yesterday may become outdated tomorrow. Businesses must deal with the recurring costs of upgrading their equipment, software, and infrastructure to stay competitive.

Security Concerns: As technology evolves, so do the tactics of cybercriminals. Protecting sensitive data from cyber threats has become a paramount concern. With each new technology comes a new vulnerability to be addressed, leading to increased pressure on IT departments and resources.

Resistance to Change: People tend to be creatures of habit, and many are resistant to change. Introducing new technologies or systems can lead to resistance, friction, and a drop in productivity as employees struggle to adapt.

Information Overload: The information age has given rise to an overwhelming volume of data. Managing this flood of information can be challenging, making it difficult to discern relevant information from the noise.

Interoperability Issues: With the plethora of technologies available, ensuring that different systems, applications, and devices work together seamlessly can be a daunting task. Incompatibility between tools can lead to inefficiencies and frustration.

Strategies for Technological Resilience

To thrive in a world where technological disruptions are the norm, businesses and individuals must embrace strategies that promote technological resilience.

1. Continuous Learning and Adaptation

Embracing technology requires a commitment to continuous learning and adaptation. This involves regular training, staying updated on industry trends, and fostering a culture of curiosity and exploration. Encouraging employees to develop new skills and adapt to emerging technologies can lead to a more agile and resilient workforce.

2. Robust Cybersecurity Measures

With cyber threats constantly evolving, a robust cybersecurity strategy is non-negotiable. Employ the latest security technologies, conduct regular security audits, and ensure employees are well-versed in cybersecurity best practices. Investing in robust security measures can prevent costly data breaches and downtime.

3. Change Management

Addressing resistance to change is crucial when implementing new technologies. Effective change management involves clear communication, involving employees in the decision-making process, and providing the necessary training and support to help them adapt. Emphasize the benefits of the new technology to motivate adoption.

4. Strategic Data Management

To combat information overload, businesses should implement strategic data management practices. This includes data classification, archiving, and leveraging data analytics to extract valuable insights. By curating the data they collect, organizations can transform it into actionable information.

5. Standardization and Compatibility

Addressing interoperability issues requires standardization and compatibility planning. Invest in technologies that are known for their compatibility with other systems. This can reduce integration challenges and enhance the overall efficiency of operations.

6. Scalable Infrastructure

To navigate the challenges of technological obsolescence, opt for scalable infrastructure. Cloud computing and virtualization allow businesses to easily expand or upgrade their systems as needed, reducing the impact of obsolescence.

7. Cross-Generational Collaboration

With multiple generations in the workforce, fostering collaboration and knowledge sharing is vital. Younger generations often bring fresh perspectives on technology, while older workers have valuable experience. Encourage mentorship programs to facilitate knowledge transfer and bridge generational gaps.

8. Agile Development and Innovation

Embracing an agile approach to development can help organizations respond to technological disruptions. Agile methodologies emphasize flexibility, iterative development, and rapid adaptation. This enables companies to respond quickly to changing circumstances and customer demands.

9. Digital Transformation Strategy

Businesses should have a well-defined digital transformation strategy. This includes a clear roadmap for adopting and integrating new technologies into the organization. Such a strategy should align with the company's overall goals and vision.

Conclusion

In the ever-evolving landscape of technology, disruptions are inevitable. However, these challenges need not be insurmountable obstacles. By implementing the right strategies, businesses and individuals can embrace technology and harness its full potential. Continuous learning and adaptation, robust cybersecurity, effective change management, strategic data management, standardization, scalability, cross-generational collaboration, agile development, and a well-defined digital transformation strategy are key pillars for dealing with technological disruptions.

The future of work is intrinsically tied to technology. Those who can navigate and thrive amidst technological disruptions will be better equipped to succeed in the modern office environment. Embracing technology is not merely about acquiring new tools; it is a mindset that values innovation, adaptation, and a commitment to growth.

In this age of technological disruption, the ability to embrace change and leverage technology is what sets apart the leaders from the followers. As we move forward in the digital era, those who apply these strategies for technological resilience will be better positioned to overcome office challenges and achieve long-term success.

Introduction

In today's dynamic and fast-paced business environment, the workplace is a melting pot of diverse personalities, perspectives, and ideas. While this diversity can lead to innovation and growth, it can also give rise to interpersonal conflicts that, if not properly managed, can disrupt the harmony and productivity of an organization. This article explores the critical topic of managing interpersonal conflicts in the workplace, highlighting the significance of effective communication and various conflict resolution techniques to foster a harmonious work environment.

Conflicts in the workplace are inevitable. They can arise from differences in personalities, work styles, or even external stressors. What's important is how these conflicts are managed. A harmonious workplace is one where employees are encouraged to resolve their disputes effectively, fostering a healthy work environment where employees can thrive and organizations can prosper.

Managing interpersonal conflicts requires a proactive approach, and it often starts with effective communication. Open and honest communication is the cornerstone of any harmonious workplace. However, communication alone isn't enough. Understanding, empathy, and the implementation of conflict resolution techniques play equally vital roles in conflict management.

The Importance of Effective Communication

1. Building Trust

Trust is the foundation of effective communication in the workplace. When employees trust each other and their leaders, they are more likely to engage in open and honest discussions. Trusting colleagues are also more willing to admit their mistakes, share their concerns, and work towards resolution, making conflicts easier to address.

2. Promoting Transparency

Transparency in communication helps prevent misunderstandings and miscommunications that can lead to conflicts. When employees and management are forthcoming with information, expectations, and feedback, it becomes easier to identify and address potential issues before they escalate into conflicts.

3. Active Listening

Listening is a crucial component of effective communication. When employees actively listen to each other's perspectives, it not only fosters understanding but also validates each person's point of view. This, in turn, promotes a sense of respect and reduces the likelihood of conflicts arising from miscommunication or misinterpretation.

4. Clear and Constructive Feedback

Providing clear and constructive feedback is essential for avoiding conflicts related to job performance. Constructive criticism should focus on behaviors and outcomes rather than personal attributes. Employees should feel that feedback is intended to help them improve, not criticize them personally.

5. Conflict Resolution Through Communication

Communication should not be seen as the source of conflict but as the key to resolving it. Encourage employees to communicate openly about their concerns and disagreements. Constructive dialogues can often lead to mutually agreeable solutions, and can also help identify common ground in areas where conflicts seem insurmountable.

Conflict Resolution Techniques

1. Mediation

Mediation involves a neutral third party who helps conflicting parties work through their differences. This third party does not make decisions but facilitates the resolution process. Mediation is an effective technique when emotions run high and individuals are unable to find common ground.

2. Collaborative Problem-Solving

Collaborative problem-solving encourages conflicting parties to work together to find a solution. This technique focuses on finding common interests and developing win-win solutions. By emphasizing cooperation and common goals, collaborative problem-solving can transform conflicts into opportunities for innovation and growth.

3. Conflict Coaching

Conflict coaching is a one-on-one process where a trained coach helps an individual navigate a conflict situation. This technique can be valuable when one party feels uncomfortable addressing the conflict directly or when there's a need to develop personal conflict resolution skills.

4. Arbitration

Arbitration involves a neutral third party who reviews the evidence and arguments presented by both sides and makes a binding decision. While it may not be the preferred method for all conflicts, it can be effective when a quick and final resolution is necessary.

5. Constructive Feedback

Providing feedback as part of conflict resolution is crucial. Feedback should be specific, based on observations, and focused on behaviors and outcomes. It should also be given with the intention of fostering growth and development, rather than assigning blame.

6. Establishing Clear Procedures

Having clear conflict resolution procedures in place can help employees feel more confident in addressing conflicts. These procedures should outline the steps to follow when conflicts arise, ensuring consistency and fairness in the resolution process.

7. Training and Development

Investing in conflict resolution training and development programs for employees and managers can help build essential skills in conflict management. These programs can include communication training, conflict resolution techniques, and strategies for building a harmonious workplace.

Conclusion

Managing interpersonal conflicts is an essential aspect of creating a harmonious workplace. Conflict, if handled effectively, can lead to growth and innovation. However, if ignored or mismanaged, it can disrupt productivity, erode trust, and lead to a toxic work environment.

Effective communication is the cornerstone of conflict management. Trust, transparency, active listening, and clear feedback are all essential components of open and honest communication. When conflicts do arise, a variety of conflict resolution techniques can be employed, from mediation and arbitration to collaborative problem-solving and constructive feedback.

To overcome office challenges and create a harmonious workplace, organizations must proactively address conflicts, foster a culture of open communication, and provide the necessary training and support to help employees and managers navigate disputes effectively. By doing so, businesses can not only resolve conflicts but also transform them into opportunities for growth and collaboration, ultimately ensuring the success and well-being of their employees and the organization as a whole.

Introduction

In today's fast-paced and demanding work environment, mastering the art of time management is an essential skill for personal and professional success. Whether you are an entry-level employee or a seasoned executive, effective time management can significantly impact your productivity, job satisfaction, and overall well-being. This article explores the key components of time management mastery and offers practical approaches to help you overcome office challenges and excel in your career.

The Art of Time Management

Time management is not just a set of tools and techniques; it's a mindset and a way of life. It's about making conscious choices, setting priorities, and aligning your actions with your goals. Here's how you can master the art of time management:

1. Setting Clear Goals and Priorities

The first step in effective time management is defining your goals and priorities. What do you want to achieve in your professional life? By having a clear sense of your objectives, you can structure your tasks and activities accordingly. Take the time to create a list of short-term and long-term goals, and review and update them regularly.

2. Time Tracking and Analysis

Before you can effectively manage your time, you need to understand how you currently spend it. Consider tracking your activities for a week, noting how much time you devote to different tasks. This exercise will reveal patterns and areas where you may be wasting time. Use tools such as time-tracking apps or simple spreadsheets to help with this analysis.

3. Efficient Task Planning

Once you have a better grasp of how you spend your time, create a daily or weekly schedule. Break your workday into blocks of time, each dedicated to specific tasks or projects. Prioritize your most important and challenging tasks during your peak energy hours, which is typically in the morning for most people. Remember to allocate some buffer time for unexpected interruptions and emergencies.

4. The Power of To-Do Lists

To-do lists are a fundamental tool in time management. They help you keep track of tasks, organize your work, and provide a sense of accomplishment when you tick off completed items. Be realistic about what you can achieve in a day and focus on quality over quantity. Consider using digital to-do list apps or traditional pen and paper, depending on your preference.

5. Delegate and Outsource

You don't have to do everything yourself. Effective leaders and professionals understand the importance of delegation. Identify tasks that others can handle and delegate them to appropriate team members. Delegating not only frees up your time but also empowers your colleagues and promotes collaboration.

6. Avoid Multitasking

Contrary to popular belief, multitasking is not a time management superpower. It divides your attention and often leads to lower quality work. Instead, focus on one task at a time. Complete it, then move on to the next. This method not only increases your efficiency but also reduces stress and improves the quality of your output.

Practical Approaches to Boost Productivity

Now that you've grasped the fundamental principles of time management, it's time to explore practical approaches to boost productivity and overcome common office challenges.

1. Time Blocks and Pomodoro Technique

One effective strategy is to use time blocks and the Pomodoro Technique. Time blocks involve dedicating a set period (e.g., 25 minutes) to a specific task, followed by a short break. This method keeps you focused and prevents burnout. It's especially useful for tasks that require deep concentration.

2. Technology and Automation

Leverage technology and automation tools to streamline routine tasks. Calendar apps can send you reminders for appointments and deadlines, while email filters can help you prioritize and organize your inbox. Consider using project management software for team collaboration and tracking progress.

3. Learn to Say No

In an office environment, it's common to be bombarded with requests and invitations to various meetings and events. While networking and collaboration are important, it's equally vital to learn to say no when necessary. Politely decline commitments that do not align with your goals or add significant value to your work.

4. Handle Distractions Effectively

Distractions are one of the biggest challenges in the modern workplace. Identify common distractions, such as social media, excessive emails, or noisy coworkers, and take measures to address them. Use website blockers or apps that limit your access to distracting sites during work hours. Communicate with colleagues about the importance of minimizing interruptions when you're deeply focused.

5. The Two-Minute Rule

Author David Allen introduced the two-minute rule in his book "Getting Things Done." If a task can be completed in two minutes or less, do it immediately. This rule prevents small tasks from piling up on your to-do list, allowing you to focus on more substantial projects.

6. Regular Breaks and Self-Care

Taking regular breaks is crucial for maintaining productivity and preventing burnout. Short breaks between tasks and a longer break for lunch can refresh your mind and improve overall performance. Additionally, prioritize self-care, including exercise, sleep, and a balanced diet, as these factors significantly affect your ability to manage time effectively.

The office landscape is continually evolving, with new technologies and challenges emerging regularly. To stay ahead, commit to continuous learning and adaptation. Attend workshops, seminars, and webinars on time management and other relevant skills. Stay updated with the latest productivity tools and methods to maintain your time management mastery.

Conclusion

Time management mastery is not a one-size-fits-all solution. It's a personalized journey that requires self-awareness, dedication, and a commitment to ongoing improvement. By setting clear goals, tracking your time, and employing practical approaches, you can overcome common office challenges and enhance your productivity.

In a world where the demands of work can be overwhelming, time management serves as a guiding light, helping you make the most of your precious hours. It allows you to work smarter, not harder, and ultimately achieve a better work-life balance. Time management mastery is not just a skill; it's a gateway to greater success, satisfaction, and a more fulfilling professional life.

Introduction

The modern workplace can be a challenging and demanding environment, often pushing employees to their limits. The pursuit of success, relentless competition, and the ever-increasing demands of the job can all contribute to the rising levels of stress and burnout. In this article, we will delve into the multifaceted issue of stress and burnout, exploring what they are, how to recognize their signs, and most importantly, how to address them effectively. As employees, managers, and employers, it is crucial to understand and manage stress and burnout in order to create a healthier, more productive, and more sustainable work environment. This article aims to provide insights and guidance for navigating the treacherous waters of workplace stress and burnout.

Understanding Stress and Burnout

Stress and burnout are often used interchangeably, but they are distinct yet related concepts. Stress is the body's natural response to a perceived threat or demand, often referred to as the "fight or flight" response. In the workplace, stress can be triggered by tight deadlines, heavy workloads, conflicts, or any other situation that makes an individual feel pressured. Stress, in moderation, can be beneficial, as it can motivate individuals to perform at their best. However, when stress becomes chronic or excessive, it can lead to burnout.

Burnout, on the other hand, is a state of chronic physical and emotional exhaustion, often accompanied by a sense of cynicism, detachment from work, and reduced performance. It's a more severe and prolonged form of stress. Burnout occurs when the demands of the job consistently exceed an individual's ability to cope, leading to a sense of hopelessness and despair.

Recognizing the Signs of Stress

Recognizing the signs of stress is the first step in preventing it from escalating into full-blown burnout. While stress manifests differently in individuals, there are common physical, emotional, and behavioral signs that can help identify when stress is becoming a problem. Some of these signs include:

1. Physical Symptoms

- Frequent headaches or migraines.
- Muscle tension and aches.
- Fatigue and low energy levels.
- Sleep disturbances, including insomnia or oversleeping.
- Digestive problems, such as stomachaches or irritable bowel syndrome.

2. Emotional Symptoms

- Anxiety and excessive worry.
- Irritability and mood swings.
- Feelings of sadness or depression.
- Difficulty in concentrating and making decisions.
- A sense of overwhelm and helplessness.

3. Behavioral Symptoms

- Increased use of alcohol or other substances as a coping mechanism.
- Social withdrawal and reduced interaction with colleagues.
- Procrastination or decreased productivity.
- Neglecting self-care, including poor eating habits and lack of exercise.

Recognizing the Signs of Burnout

Burnout is often the result of prolonged exposure to chronic stress. While the signs of burnout can overlap with stress, there are specific indicators that point to a more severe problem. Recognizing these signs is essential for early intervention. Some common signs of burnout include:

1. Physical and Emotional Exhaustion

- Constant fatigue, even after a good night's sleep.
- Feeling emotionally drained and detached from work or personal life.
- Frequent physical symptoms like headaches and stomach issues.

2. Reduced Performance and Productivity

- Decreased work performance and productivity.
- A sense of disillusionment with work, colleagues, and clients.
- Difficulty concentrating and making decisions.

3. Increased Cynicism and Detachment

- Growing cynicism and negativity about the job and workplace.
- Social withdrawal and decreased engagement with colleagues.
- A feeling of isolation and disconnection.

4. Loss of Personal Identity

- A loss of a sense of purpose and personal identity linked to one's job.
- A shift in personal values and priorities.

Safeguarding Mental and Emotional Well-being

Recognizing the signs of stress and burnout is essential, but it's equally important to take proactive steps to safeguard mental and emotional well-being in the workplace. Here are some strategies for addressing stress and preventing burnout:

Time Management: One of the leading causes of workplace stress is the feeling of being overwhelmed by tasks and deadlines. Effective time management can help employees prioritize their work, set achievable goals, and reduce stress.

Set Realistic Expectations: Both employees and employers should set realistic expectations for job performance. Unrealistic expectations can lead to stress and burnout, while achievable goals can boost motivation and job satisfaction.

Work-Life Balance: Encouraging a healthy work-life balance is crucial in preventing burnout. Employers can promote flexible work arrangements, while employees should make an effort to unplug from work when not on the clock.

Mental Health Support: Companies should invest in mental health programs and resources for employees. This can include access to counselors, stress management workshops, and support groups.

Clear Communication: Effective communication between managers and employees is key to preventing burnout. Employees should feel comfortable discussing their concerns, and managers should be receptive and empathetic.

Self-Care: Employees should prioritize self-care by getting regular exercise, maintaining a balanced diet, and practicing relaxation techniques like meditation and mindfulness.

Social Support: Building strong relationships with colleagues can provide a crucial support system in times of stress. Social support can mitigate the negative effects of workplace stress.

Time Off: Encourage employees to take regular time off to recharge. Vacation and personal days are essential for maintaining mental and emotional well-being.

Conclusion

In a world where the pressure to succeed often overshadows the importance of mental and emotional well-being, recognizing and addressing the signs of stress and burnout is of paramount importance. This article has shed light on the distinct yet interconnected concepts of stress and burnout, highlighted their signs, and provided strategies for safeguarding mental and emotional well-being in the workplace.

Stress is a natural response to the demands of modern work, but when left unmanaged, it can lead to burnout, a debilitating condition that affects both the individual and the organization. By understanding the signs of stress and burnout and taking proactive steps to address them, employees, managers, and employers can create a healthier, more sustainable work environment where individuals can thrive both professionally and personally.

In the end, the well-being of employees is not just a matter of ethics; it's also a strategic imperative. A mentally and emotionally healthy workforce is more engaged, productive, and innovative, contributing to the success of the organization. Therefore, recognizing and addressing stress and burnout is not just a matter of individual health but a business imperative that should be woven into the fabric of every workplace culture.

Introduction

The modern workplace is an intricate ecosystem filled with various challenges and stressors that can significantly impact an individual's mental health. For many people, the office environment becomes a source of stress, anxiety, and even depression. This article explores the mental health implications of office challenges and provides a comprehensive set of strategies for maintaining a healthy mind. We will delve into the various stressors that can affect employees, discuss the importance of mental health at work, and offer actionable steps to promote well-being. In a world where work is an integral part of our lives, ensuring mental health at the office is of paramount importance.

Mental Health Implications of Office Challenges

1. The Pressure to Perform

One of the most significant stressors in the workplace is the pressure to perform. Employees are often under constant scrutiny to meet deadlines, exceed targets, and demonstrate their value. This pressure can lead to feelings of inadequacy, anxiety, and even burnout.

To combat this challenge, it is essential to set realistic expectations, both for oneself and for employees. Employers can encourage a healthy work-life balance, provide resources for time management, and promote open communication to address concerns and provide support.

2. Workplace Bullying and Harassment

Workplace bullying and harassment can have a profound impact on mental health. When employees experience such behavior, it erodes their self-esteem, triggers anxiety and depression, and hampers their overall well-being.

To address this issue, organizations must establish clear anti-bullying and harassment policies and provide training to employees and management. Creating a culture of respect and inclusivity is vital to combatting these challenges.

3. Long Working Hours

The culture of long working hours is pervasive in many workplaces, leading to physical and mental exhaustion. Extended work hours can disrupt one's work-life balance, leading to stress and strained relationships.

Employers should actively promote and encourage reasonable working hours and offer flexibility when possible. Additionally, teaching employees time management techniques and the importance of setting boundaries can help mitigate the negative impact of long working hours.

4. Lack of Job Security

Uncertainty regarding job security is another significant stressor in the workplace. The fear of job loss can lead to chronic anxiety and negatively impact an employee's mental health.

To address this, companies should provide transparency and open communication about job stability. Offering employees opportunities for upskilling and reskilling can enhance their confidence in the face of job insecurity. *Upskilling* refers to acquiring new skills or enhancing existing ones, while *reskilling* involves learning entirely new skills to adapt to changing job requirements or career shifts.

5. Isolation and Loneliness

The rise of remote work, while offering flexibility, has also brought forth challenges in the form of isolation and loneliness. Many employees struggle with feelings of disconnection and a lack of social interaction.

To combat this, organizations should focus on fostering a sense of community, even among remote employees. Virtual team-building activities, regular video conferences, and open channels for communication can help alleviate isolation.

6. Unrealistic Expectations and Perfectionism

Some individuals hold themselves to exceptionally high standards, often driven by the fear of making mistakes or disappointing others. This perfectionism can result in anxiety, low self-esteem, and excessive stress.

Employers should emphasize a growth mindset and create a culture that encourages learning from mistakes. Providing regular feedback and recognizing that imperfections are a part of the growth process can help individuals let go of unrealistic expectations.

Strategies for Maintaining a Healthy Mind

1. Self-awareness and Self-care

The foundation of good mental health in the office begins with self-awareness. Employees must recognize their stressors, triggers, and emotional responses. Self-awareness allows individuals to take proactive steps to manage their mental health effectively.

Self-care practices, such as regular exercise, a balanced diet, and adequate sleep, are essential components of well-being. Additionally, mindfulness and meditation techniques can help individuals manage stress and stay grounded.

2. Open Communication

Promoting open communication in the workplace is crucial for addressing mental health challenges. Employees should feel comfortable discussing their concerns with their supervisors and colleagues. Likewise, employers should create an environment that encourages such dialogues.

Mental health awareness campaigns, workshops, and access to confidential counseling services can destigmatize mental health conversations and provide support to those in need.

3. Work-life Balance

A healthy work-life balance is essential for maintaining good mental health. Employees should set boundaries and allocate time for personal activities and relaxation. Employers can support this by encouraging employees to use their allotted time off and avoiding after-hours expectations.

4. Training and Education

Educating employees about mental health is another key strategy. Organizations can provide training on stress management, emotional intelligence, and resilience-building. This equips employees with the tools to navigate office challenges and maintain their mental health effectively.

5. Supportive Work Environment

A supportive work environment is one where employees feel valued, appreciated, and recognized for their contributions. Recognizing employees' efforts and achievements can boost morale and contribute to a positive atmosphere.

Employers can also provide flexible work arrangements, such as remote work options and flexible hours, to accommodate various needs and preferences. Additionally, creating dedicated spaces for relaxation and meditation within the office can encourage stress relief.

6. Anti-bullying and Harassment Policies

To combat workplace bullying and harassment, organizations must establish strict policies and consequences for such behaviors. Training programs should be implemented to educate employees on what constitutes harassment and how to report it. Additionally, offering support to victims and ensuring their confidentiality is maintained can help them cope with the trauma.

7. Job Security

To address the fear of job insecurity, employers should provide clear communication about the organization's stability and future prospects. Offering opportunities for professional development and advancement can also instill confidence in employees.

8. Social Interaction

To mitigate the effects of isolation and loneliness, companies should invest in virtual team-building activities, regular check-ins, and group projects. Creating a sense of belonging and shared goals can enhance social interaction among remote workers.

9. Mindfulness and Resilience Training

Teaching employees mindfulness and resilience techniques can help them manage stress and maintain mental health. These strategies enable individuals to stay focused, calm, and adaptable in the face of challenges.

Conclusion

Mental health and the office are intertwined in ways that cannot be ignored. Office challenges, whether they stem from pressure to perform, workplace bullying, long working hours, or a lack of job security, can have profound implications for an individual's mental well-being. However, with the right strategies, individuals and organizations can promote and maintain mental health in the workplace.

The importance of self-awareness, self-care, open communication, and work-life balance cannot be overstated. Employees must recognize their mental health needs and be proactive in seeking help and support when necessary. Employers, in turn, should prioritize mental health awareness, create a supportive work environment, and offer training and education to equip their workforce with the tools needed to navigate office challenges.

In today's fast-paced, competitive world, well-being in the office is a collective responsibility. By addressing mental health challenges and implementing strategies for maintaining a healthy mind, both individuals and organizations can contribute to a happier, more productive, and mentally healthy workforce. In doing so, they not only improve the quality of work but also the quality of life for everyone involved.

Chapter 7. Physical Health in the Workplace
Overcoming the Risks

Introduction

In today's fast-paced and technology-driven world, office work has become a significant part of our daily lives. We spend long hours at our desks, staring at screens, attending meetings, and tackling endless tasks. While the modern workplace has brought about tremendous efficiency and convenience, it has also given rise to several challenges concerning physical health. The sedentary nature of office work, combined with the stress and pressure it often entails, can have adverse effects on our well-being. This article explores the physical health consequences of office work and offers valuable tips for maintaining a healthy lifestyle in the workplace.

The modern workplace is a hub of productivity and innovation, but it is not without its drawbacks, particularly when it comes to physical health. The sedentary nature of office work, which requires extended periods of sitting at a desk, can take a toll on our bodies. Coupled with the stress, pressure, and often unhealthy lifestyle habits that come with the job, the risks to our physical well-being are substantial. However, with the right strategies and a proactive approach, we can overcome these challenges and maintain good health while excelling in our professional lives.

Physical Health Consequences of Office Work

1. Sedentary Lifestyle and Its Effects

One of the most significant health risks associated with office work is the sedentary lifestyle it promotes. People spend an average of 8-9 hours a day sitting at their desks, which can have detrimental effects on the body. Prolonged sitting can lead to a range of health issues, including:

Obesity: A sedentary lifestyle contributes to weight gain and obesity. The lack of physical activity reduces calorie expenditure and can lead to an imbalance between calories consumed and calories burned.

Muscle Atrophy: Extended sitting can result in the weakening and atrophy of muscles, particularly those in the back, legs, and core. This can lead to poor posture and musculoskeletal problems.

Cardiovascular Problems: Prolonged sitting is associated with an increased risk of heart disease. It can lead to higher levels of cholesterol and blood pressure, which are risk factors for cardiovascular issues.

2. Ergonomic Challenges

Many office workers face ergonomic challenges that can affect their physical health. Poorly designed workstations, uncomfortable chairs, and improper desk setups can lead to various issues, including:

Back Pain: Improper seating and desk ergonomics can cause back pain, which is a common complaint among office workers.

Carpal Tunnel Syndrome: Improper keyboard and mouse positioning can contribute to carpal tunnel syndrome, which affects the wrists and hands. *Carpal Tunnel Syndrome* (CTS) is a common medical condition that causes numbness, tingling, and weakness in the hand and wrist due to the compression of the median nerve as it passes through the carpal tunnel in the wrist.

Eye Strain: Staring at screens for extended periods can lead to eye strain, headaches, and even long-term vision problems.

3. Stress and Mental Health Impacts

Stress is a prevalent feature of office work, and it can have a profound impact on both mental and physical health. Chronic stress can lead to various health issues, such as:

Increased Cortisol Levels: High levels of stress can lead to an overproduction of cortisol, a hormone associated with weight gain and inflammation.

Anxiety and Depression: The pressure and demands of office work can contribute to mental health issues, including anxiety and depression.

Weakened Immune System: Prolonged stress weakens the immune system, making individuals more susceptible to illnesses.

4. Unhealthy Eating Habits

The workplace can also be a breeding ground for unhealthy eating habits. Busy schedules, tight deadlines, and readily available office snacks can lead to poor dietary choices. Common issues include:

Overeating: Stress can lead to emotional eating, causing individuals to overeat, particularly unhealthy foods high in sugar and fat.

Lack of Nutrient-Rich Foods: Office workers may neglect to consume a balanced diet rich in fruits, vegetables, and whole grains, which can lead to nutrient deficiencies.

Weight Gain: Unhealthy eating habits can result in weight gain, further exacerbating the physical health risks associated with office work.

Tips for Maintaining a Healthy Lifestyle

Now that we've explored the physical health consequences of office work, let's discuss effective strategies for overcoming these risks and promoting a healthier lifestyle in the workplace.

1. Incorporate Physical Activity

Breaking up long periods of sitting with short bursts of physical activity can make a significant difference. Here are some tips to incorporate physical activity into your workday:

Desk Exercises: Perform simple desk exercises like seated leg raises, desk push-ups, or stretching to keep your muscles engaged.

Walk Breaks: Take short walks around the office or outside during your breaks. This can help improve circulation and reduce the negative effects of prolonged sitting.

Standing Desk: If possible, use a standing desk for part of your workday. This can alleviate the strain on your back and legs.

2. Ergonomic Workspace Setup

Ensure that your workspace is ergonomically designed to minimize the risk of physical health issues. Consider the following:

Proper Chair and Desk Height: Adjust your chair and desk to ensure that your feet are flat on the ground and your arms are at a 90-degree angle when typing.

Monitor Position: Position your monitor at eye level to reduce strain on your neck and eyes.

Ergonomic Accessories: Invest in ergonomic accessories, such as an ergonomic chair, keyboard, and mouse, to improve comfort and reduce the risk of injury.

3. Stress Management

Dealing with stress is crucial for maintaining both mental and physical health. Here are some stress management techniques:

Time Management: Effectively manage your time by setting priorities, creating to-do lists, and breaking tasks into manageable chunks.

Mindfulness and Meditation: Practice mindfulness and meditation techniques to reduce stress levels and promote mental well-being.

Work-Life Balance: **Maintain a healthy work-life balance by setting boundaries and disconnecting from work when off the clock.**

4. Healthy Eating Habits

Promoting healthy eating habits in the workplace can go a long way in preventing weight gain and other related health issues:

Meal Prepping: **Prepare healthy meals and snacks at home to bring to the office. This can help you avoid unhealthy office snacks and takeout options.**

Stay Hydrated: **Drink plenty of water throughout the day to stay hydrated and prevent mindless snacking.**

Avoid Sugary and Processed Foods: **Limit your consumption of sugary and processed foods in the office. Opt for healthier options like fruits, vegetables, and whole grains.**

5. Regular Health Checkups

Regular health checkups are essential for monitoring your physical health. Consider the following:

Annual Physical Exams: **Schedule annual checkups with your healthcare provider to assess your overall health and catch any issues early.**

Eyesight and Hearing Tests: **Regularly check your eyesight and hearing to ensure you're not straining your eyes or ears.**

Ergonomic Assessments: Seek an ergonomic assessment at work to ensure your workspace is set up to support your physical well-being.

6. Encourage a Healthy Workplace Culture

Promoting a healthy workplace culture benefits not only individuals but the entire organization. Encourage your colleagues and superiors to adopt these practices:

Wellness Programs: Advocate for workplace wellness programs that offer fitness classes, stress management workshops, and health challenges.

Healthy Office Snacks: Suggest providing healthier snack options in the office kitchen or vending machines.

Flexible Work Arrangements: Encourage flexible work arrangements that allow for remote work, standing desks, or alternative work hours.

Conclusion

Physical health in the workplace is a matter of paramount importance. The sedentary nature of office work, coupled with stress and unhealthy lifestyle habits, can pose significant risks to our well-being. However, by incorporating physical activity, optimizing our workspace, managing stress, adopting healthy eating habits, scheduling regular health checkups, and promoting a healthy workplace culture, we can overcome these risks and enjoy a healthier and more productive work life.

Striking a balance between professional success and personal health is not only possible but necessary. In doing so, we can lead fulfilling, productive lives while safeguarding our physical well-being in the modern workplace. Remember, your health is your most valuable asset, and with the right strategies, you can protect and enhance it even in the midst of office challenges.

Introduction

In today's fast-paced and demanding work environments, the ability to effectively manage oneself is a crucial skill. The concept of self-management revolves around taking control of your work life, making the most of your time, and achieving your professional goals. In this article, we will explore self-management techniques and strategies to help you overcome the many challenges faced in the modern workplace. By mastering the art of self-management, you can become more productive, reduce stress, and enhance your overall work-life balance.

Goal Setting and Prioritization

One of the fundamental pillars of self-management is setting clear and achievable goals. Effective goal setting provides a roadmap for your work life, helping you stay focused and motivated. Here are some key considerations when setting and prioritizing your goals:

SMART Goals: SMART stands for Specific, Measurable, Achievable, Relevant, and Time-bound. When setting your goals, make sure they meet these criteria. Specific goals provide clarity, measurable goals allow you to track progress, achievable goals ensure they are within your capabilities, relevant goals align with your broader objectives, and time-bound goals create a sense of urgency.

Long-Term vs. Short-Term Goals: Distinguish between long-term and short-term goals. Long-term goals are your overarching objectives, while short-term goals are the smaller, incremental steps you take to reach those long-term goals. Prioritize your short-term goals to make steady progress toward your larger aspirations.

Prioritization: Not all goals are created equal. Identify your most important and urgent goals and prioritize them accordingly. This approach ensures that you tackle the most critical tasks first, preventing procrastination and fostering a sense of accomplishment.

The Eisenhower Matrix: The Eisenhower Matrix, also known as the Urgent-Important Matrix, helps in prioritizing tasks. It classifies tasks into four categories: urgent and important, not urgent but important, urgent but not important, and neither urgent nor important. Focus on the important tasks, regardless of their urgency.

Effective Planning and Organization

Once you've established your goals and priorities, effective planning and organization are essential for self-management. These strategies will help you make the most of your time and resources:

Time Management: Time is a finite resource, and effective time management is crucial. Tools like time tracking apps and calendars can help you schedule your day, allocate time to specific tasks, and minimize time-wasting activities.

To-Do Lists: Create daily or weekly to-do lists to keep track of tasks. Breaking down your goals into smaller, actionable steps makes them more manageable and less overwhelming. Cross items off the list as you complete them for a sense of achievement.

Batch Processing: Batch processing involves grouping similar tasks together and working on them during designated time blocks. For example, you can set aside a specific time to respond to emails, make phone calls, or tackle creative work. This minimizes context-switching and boosts productivity.

Technology Tools: Embrace technology to help with organization. Project management software, task management apps, and cloud storage solutions can streamline your work processes and keep your information accessible and secure.

Declutter Your Workspace: A cluttered workspace can be distracting and hinder your productivity. Regularly declutter your workspace to create a clean, organized environment that fosters focus and creativity.

Delegation: Understand that you don't have to do everything yourself. Delegating tasks to colleagues or team members can free up your time to focus on more critical responsibilities. Effective delegation is a skill that can reduce your workload and increase your efficiency.

Time Blocking: Time blocking involves allocating specific time slots for different types of tasks. For example, you can dedicate the morning to focused work, the afternoon to meetings, and the evening to administrative tasks. This method ensures that each aspect of your work receives dedicated attention.

Learn to Say No: One of the challenges in self-management is the temptation to overcommit. Learn to say no when additional tasks or projects will overwhelm your schedule. Prioritize your existing commitments and only take on new responsibilities when you have the capacity.

Conclusion

Self-management is the key to success in a busy work life. By setting clear goals and priorities, and then planning and organizing effectively, you can take control of your work life and make it more productive and less stressful. In conclusion, here are some key takeaways:

Goal setting is the foundation of self-management. Use SMART goals, differentiate between long-term and short-term goals, and prioritize effectively.

Time management and to-do lists are crucial tools for daily organization. Make the most of your time by batch processing, using technology, decluttering your workspace, and learning to say no when necessary.

Effective planning and organization are ongoing processes. Be adaptable and open to refining your self-management techniques as your work life evolves.

Self-management is a skill that can be learned and refined over time. It will help you not only achieve your professional goals but also improve your work-life balance and overall well-being.

Remember that self-management is a continuous journey, and the techniques and strategies discussed in this article can be adapted to suit your unique work-life challenges. Embrace self-management as a way to regain control, reduce stress, and achieve your career aspirations. With the right mindset and dedication, you can navigate the complexities of the modern workplace with confidence and success.

Introduction

In the modern workplace, challenges are inevitable. From navigating the complexities of remote work to managing diverse teams, today's office environment is rife with obstacles that can hinder productivity and hinder employee well-being. However, in the face of these challenges, effective leadership plays a critical role in steering the ship through troubled waters. This article delves into the multifaceted role of leadership in overcoming office challenges and explores how they can transform hurdles into opportunities. By fostering a supportive work environment, leaders can empower their teams to excel and thrive, no matter the difficulties they face.

Effective Leadership in Addressing Challenges

1. Vision and Direction

Effective leaders provide clarity and direction to their teams, even in the face of uncertainty and change. They set a vision for the organization and communicate it clearly to employees. By defining a compelling mission and setting achievable goals, leaders can rally their teams around a common purpose. This unifies the workforce and motivates them to tackle challenges with a shared sense of purpose.

2. Adaptability

In a rapidly evolving business landscape, leaders must be adaptable and open to change. They need to embrace new technologies and approaches, showing their teams that they are willing to evolve and grow. An adaptable leader encourages a culture of innovation and resilience, making it easier for the office to confront and conquer challenges head-on.

3. Decision-Making

Leaders are often required to make tough decisions, especially when facing challenges that impact the office. Sound decision-making is a cornerstone of effective leadership. Leaders must gather information, consider the consequences, and act decisively. Their ability to make the right calls, even in challenging situations, can be the difference between overcoming obstacles or succumbing to them.

4. Communication

Open and transparent communication is essential for navigating office challenges. Leaders must maintain regular dialogue with their teams, sharing updates, addressing concerns, and providing support. Effective communication fosters trust and ensures that everyone is on the same page, working together to find solutions.

5. Resilience

Challenges can be demoralizing, but leaders can set an example by demonstrating resilience. In the face of adversity, they should remain steadfast and composed. Their ability to bounce back from setbacks and maintain a positive attitude inspires their teams to do the same, even when the odds seem stacked against them.

Fostering a Supportive Work Environment

1. Empowerment

A key aspect of effective leadership in overcoming office challenges is empowering employees. Leaders should trust their teams to make decisions and take ownership of their work. Empowered employees are more likely to seek creative solutions and persevere when confronted with difficulties. This empowerment can help teams overcome challenges with greater confidence and independence.

2. Team Building

Effective leaders recognize that the strength of a team is greater than the sum of its parts. They invest in team building activities, fostering a sense of camaraderie and mutual support among employees. A well-knit team is better equipped to face office challenges together, as they can draw upon each other's strengths and work collaboratively to find solutions.

3. Learning and Development

Leaders can encourage a culture of continuous learning and development. By providing training and growth opportunities, they equip their teams with the skills and knowledge needed to overcome challenges. Employees who are confident in their abilities are more likely to tackle difficulties with enthusiasm and resourcefulness.

4. Emotional Intelligence

Leaders with strong emotional intelligence are better at understanding and managing the emotions of their team members. They are empathetic, able to listen actively, and provide support when needed. By creating a safe and supportive emotional environment, leaders enable their teams to navigate challenges with less stress and greater resilience.

5. Conflict Resolution

Challenges can often lead to conflicts within the office. Effective leaders are skilled at conflict resolution, mediating disputes and promoting a harmonious work environment. By addressing and resolving conflicts swiftly, they prevent these issues from escalating and derailing productivity.

6. Work-Life Balance

In a world where work-life balance is crucial, leaders must advocate for it. Encouraging flexible work arrangements and time-off policies helps employees manage their personal lives, reducing stress and burnout. When employees are less overwhelmed, they are better equipped to tackle office challenges effectively.

7. Diversity and Inclusion

Diverse teams bring a broader range of perspectives and experiences to the table, making them more adept at problem-solving. Leaders should actively promote diversity and inclusion in the workplace, creating a culture where every employee feels valued and heard. This fosters creativity and innovation, enabling teams to overcome challenges with fresh ideas and approaches.

Conclusion

Leadership plays a pivotal role in overcoming office challenges. Effective leaders provide vision, adaptability, sound decision-making, and transparent communication. They are resilient in the face of adversity and set an example for their teams. Through empowerment, team building, and a focus on learning and development, leaders create an environment where employees can thrive. They leverage emotional intelligence and conflict resolution skills to maintain a harmonious workplace and prioritize work-life balance. Finally, leaders champion diversity and inclusion, harnessing the power of varied perspectives to tackle challenges creatively.

In the ever-evolving landscape of the modern workplace, leadership is the guiding force that helps organizations not just survive but thrive. Challenges will continue to arise, but with effective leadership, these challenges become opportunities for growth and development. By fostering a supportive work environment and empowering their teams, leaders pave the way for success, no matter the obstacles they face. As we continue to navigate the complexities of the contemporary office, let's remember that with strong leadership, we can conquer any challenge that comes our way.

Chapter 10. Common Challenges Across Office Roles

Introduction

Office environments are dynamic and multifaceted, comprising a diverse range of roles and responsibilities. Each role brings its own set of challenges and complexities, which can significantly impact an individual's productivity and well-being. In this article, we will explore the common challenges that individuals face across various office roles and discuss strategies to overcome them. Whether you're an administrative assistant, a manager, a creative professional, or any other member of an office team, understanding and addressing these challenges is crucial for success.

The Impact of Office Challenges on Productivity

Before delving into the specific challenges faced by different office roles, it's essential to recognize the overarching impact of these challenges on productivity. Regardless of your job title, when these challenges go unaddressed, they can hinder your ability to perform at your best. Here are some ways in which office challenges can affect productivity:

Stress and Burnout: Many office challenges, such as heavy workloads, tight deadlines, and interpersonal conflicts, can lead to stress and burnout. When employees are constantly stressed, their productivity often suffers, and they may become more prone to absenteeism and turnover.

Decreased Morale: Facing challenges without effective strategies to overcome them can lead to decreased morale.

Employees who feel undervalued or unsupported in dealing with their issues are less likely to be motivated and engaged in their work.

Reduced Efficiency: Challenges often create roadblocks that hinder the efficient completion of tasks. This can result in wasted time, duplicated efforts, and overall inefficiency in the workplace.

Communication Breakdowns: Challenges can strain communication among team members and departments. Effective communication is vital for collaboration and problem-solving, and when it breaks down, it can impede productivity.

Now, let's delve into the specific challenges faced by different office roles and explore strategies to overcome them.

Administrative and Support Staff Challenges

Heavy Workloads: Administrative and support staff often juggle a wide range of responsibilities, from managing calendars and handling correspondence to providing general office support. This can lead to heavy workloads that make it challenging to prioritize and manage tasks effectively.

Strategy: To address heavy workloads, consider implementing time management techniques, such as the Eisenhower Matrix, to prioritize tasks and delegate when necessary. It's also important to communicate with supervisors about workload concerns and explore options for additional support.

Interpersonal Conflicts: Administrative professionals frequently interact with various colleagues, which can sometimes lead to interpersonal conflicts. These conflicts can result from miscommunications, differences in work styles, or conflicting priorities.

Strategy: To navigate interpersonal conflicts, open and honest communication is key. Encourage a culture of respect and understanding within the workplace. Address conflicts promptly, listen to all parties involved, and work together to find solutions that promote harmony and productivity.

Tech Overload: In today's digital age, administrative and support staff often find themselves using a wide array of software and tools. Managing these technologies and keeping up with updates and new platforms can be overwhelming.

Strategy: Invest in training and development to enhance technology proficiency. Consider streamlining the use of technology by adopting integrated systems where possible. Regularly evaluate the necessity of various tools and eliminate redundancies.

Lack of Recognition: Support staff, despite their critical roles, may feel undervalued and underappreciated, which can lead to a decrease in motivation and job satisfaction.

Strategy: Ensure that recognition and appreciation are integrated into the workplace culture. Recognize the contributions of administrative and support staff regularly, and offer opportunities for professional growth and development.

Challenges Across Middle Management Roles

Balancing Act: Middle managers are often caught in a balancing act between meeting the demands of senior management and addressing the concerns and needs of their teams. This can create stress and conflict.

Strategy: Effective time management is essential for middle managers. Prioritize tasks and delegate responsibilities when appropriate. Open lines of communication with both higher-ups and team members to ensure a harmonious balance.

Decision-Making Pressures: Middle managers are frequently tasked with making critical decisions that can have a significant impact on the organization. The pressure to make the right choices can be daunting.

Strategy: Develop decision-making frameworks and seek input from relevant stakeholders when making important choices. Embrace a growth mindset that views decisions, even when they don't yield the desired outcomes, as opportunities for learning and improvement.

Employee Engagement: Keeping team members engaged and motivated is a continuous challenge for middle managers. Disengaged employees can affect team dynamics and overall productivity.

Strategy: Establish regular one-on-one meetings with team members to understand their goals and challenges. Create a positive and inclusive team culture, where individual contributions are valued and recognized. Provide opportunities for professional development and growth within the team.

Challenges for Creative Professionals

Creative Block: Creative professionals often experience periods of creative block, where they struggle to come up with fresh ideas or solutions for projects.

Strategy: Embrace techniques like brainstorming sessions, mind mapping, and collaboration with colleagues to overcome creative block. Create a stimulating and inspiring workspace to encourage innovation.

Tight Deadlines: Creativity can't always be rushed, but in a corporate environment, creative professionals are often under pressure to meet tight deadlines.

Strategy: Effective time management and project planning are crucial. Set realistic deadlines, communicate any concerns about timeline feasibility, and collaborate with team members to ensure a balanced workload.

Lack of Understanding: Sometimes, creative professionals may find that their work is not fully understood or appreciated by non-creative colleagues or clients.

Strategy: Educate colleagues and clients about the creative process and the value of creativity in achieving business goals. Use storytelling and examples to illustrate the impact of creative work.

Conclusion

In any office environment, challenges are inevitable, and each role comes with its unique set of issues. However, understanding these common challenges and implementing strategies to overcome them is vital for maintaining productivity and overall job satisfaction.

In this article, we've examined challenges faced by administrative and support staff, middle managers, and creative professionals. These challenges range from heavy workloads to creative blocks, and from decision-making pressures to interpersonal conflicts. While the specific challenges may differ, the overarching strategies for overcoming them often include effective communication, time management, and a focus on professional development and recognition.

It's crucial for both employees and organizations to work collaboratively in addressing these challenges. A supportive and inclusive workplace culture, ongoing training and development, and open lines of communication can go a long way in ensuring that employees at all levels can thrive in their respective roles.

Ultimately, recognizing and addressing these common challenges will lead to a more productive and harmonious office environment, benefiting both individuals and the organization as a whole.

Introduction

Sales and marketing are the driving forces behind a successful business. They are responsible for generating revenue, expanding the customer base, and ultimately ensuring the company's growth and profitability. However, the path to success in sales and marketing is often fraught with challenges that can be daunting for even the most seasoned professionals. In this article, we will delve into some of the most prevalent challenges faced in the world of sales and marketing and explore effective strategies to overcome them. By understanding and addressing these challenges, businesses can achieve their sales targets, build strong client relationships, and thrive in a competitive marketplace.

Meeting Sales Targets and Quotas

One of the most significant challenges in sales and marketing is meeting sales targets and quotas. These numerical goals serve as a benchmark for a company's performance and are often the primary metric by which success is measured. Failing to meet these targets can have serious consequences, including financial losses and a decline in morale among the sales team. To overcome this challenge, businesses must employ various strategies.

Setting Realistic Goals: The first step in overcoming sales targets and quotas challenges is to set realistic and achievable goals. Unrealistic targets can lead to frustration and demotivation among the sales team. It's essential to base these goals on historical data, market trends, and the capabilities of your sales team.

Sales Training and Development: Providing ongoing training and development opportunities for your sales team is crucial. Equipping them with the right skills and knowledge will enable them to perform more effectively. Regular training sessions, workshops, and access to sales resources can help your team stay ahead of the competition.

Sales Process Optimization: Streamlining the sales process can make a significant difference in meeting targets. Identify bottlenecks, streamline workflows, and implement automation where possible. This will increase efficiency and help your team close deals faster.

Incentives and Rewards: Implement a rewards system that recognizes and appreciates the hard work and dedication of your sales team. Incentives can be financial, such as bonuses, or non-financial, such as recognition and awards. Motivated salespeople are more likely to surpass their targets.

Data-Driven Decision-Making: Utilize data analytics to gain insights into your sales performance. By understanding customer behavior, market trends, and your team's strengths and weaknesses, you can make informed decisions and adjust your strategies accordingly.

Generating Leads and Building Client Relationships

The process of generating leads and building strong client relationships is another critical aspect of sales and marketing. Lead generation in business is the process of identifying and attracting potential customers or "leads" who have shown interest in a product or service, with the goal of nurturing and converting them into paying customers. In today's competitive business landscape, capturing the attention of potential customers and nurturing existing relationships can be challenging.

Lead Generation Challenges: Lead generation can be a stumbling block for many businesses. To address this challenge, it's essential to diversify your lead sources. Explore online and offline channels, invest in content marketing, and participate in industry events and trade shows. Moreover, consider lead nurturing strategies to keep potential customers engaged.

Quality vs. Quantity: While generating leads is important, it's equally crucial to focus on lead quality. A *lead* refers to a potential customer or individual who has shown interest in a product or service offered by a business. *Lead quality* refers to how likely these individuals are to become paying customers, with high-quality leads being those with a greater likelihood of conversion. A large number of low-quality leads can consume resources without yielding significant results. Therefore, businesses should invest in lead scoring and qualification processes to identify the most promising leads.

Building Client Relationships: Building strong and lasting client relationships is the cornerstone of successful sales and marketing. This involves continuous communication, understanding client needs, and providing personalized solutions.

Personalization and Customization: Tailoring your marketing and sales efforts to meet individual client needs can set you apart from competitors. Use data-driven insights to create personalized content and offers, and ensure that your communication is relevant to each client.

Active Listening: Active listening is a fundamental skill in building client relationships. By paying close attention to your clients' concerns, questions, and feedback, you can show them that you genuinely care about their needs and are willing to address them.

Value-Added Services: Go beyond the transactional aspect of sales and provide value-added services that demonstrate your commitment to the client's success. This could include ongoing support, educational resources, or additional features and benefits.

Conclusion

In the ever-evolving world of sales and marketing, challenges are inevitable. However, they should not be viewed as insurmountable obstacles but rather as opportunities for growth and improvement. By setting realistic sales targets, providing continuous training, and streamlining processes, businesses can enhance their chances of meeting quotas and achieving success.

Lead generation and client relationship building can be challenging, but diversifying lead sources, focusing on lead quality, and personalized approaches can significantly improve results. Ultimately, the success of any sales and marketing team depends on its ability to adapt, learn from past experiences, and continually evolve to meet the demands of the market.

In conclusion, facing and overcoming these challenges is essential for the success of any sales and marketing team. With the right strategies, a commitment to improvement, and a dedicated team, businesses can rise above the obstacles and thrive in a competitive marketplace. Sales and marketing are dynamic fields that require constant attention and innovation, and those who adapt and excel will find themselves well-positioned for long-term success.

Introduction

In today's digital age, information technology (IT) plays a pivotal role in almost every aspect of business operations. From managing data and communication to enhancing productivity and customer service, IT is an indispensable part of modern office environments. However, with the increasing reliance on technology comes a plethora of IT and technical support challenges. This article explores these challenges in depth, discussing the complexities that IT professionals face in the workplace and strategies to overcome them.

Handling Technical Issues and User Complaints

1. The Complex Web of Technical Issues

Technical issues are an inevitable part of working with IT. These problems can range from minor inconveniences, like a malfunctioning printer, to major system-wide outages. IT professionals are tasked with diagnosing and resolving these issues efficiently to ensure minimal disruption to the workflow.

One of the major challenges in this area is the vast array of devices, software, and configurations used in the modern office. Each variation can present a unique set of problems. For instance, a Mac user might experience issues that are entirely different from those faced by a PC user. The diversity of the IT environment requires IT support teams to be well-versed in various platforms, which can be overwhelming.

To address this challenge, companies often implement comprehensive knowledge bases and documentation. These resources aid IT professionals in troubleshooting and resolving issues faster. Additionally, the use of remote support tools allows IT teams to address problems without having to be physically present, saving time and resources.

2. User Complaints and Expectations

Users often feel frustrated when technical issues disrupt their work, and handling user complaints is another significant challenge for IT professionals. Users typically expect quick resolutions to their problems and can sometimes express their frustration in various ways, making it challenging for support staff to manage their emotions while addressing technical issues.

To tackle this challenge, IT professionals need not only technical expertise but also excellent communication and interpersonal skills. Active listening, patience, and the ability to empathize with the users' situations are crucial. Establishing a user-friendly ticketing system and providing regular updates on the status of their issues can go a long way in managing user expectations and reducing frustration.

Staying Updated with Technology and Cybersecurity

1. Rapid Technological Advancements

Technology evolves at a rapid pace, introducing new software, hardware, and tools regularly. This continual evolution presents IT professionals with the challenge of staying updated with the latest advancements to provide effective support. Falling behind in technological knowledge can lead to inefficiency and errors in resolving technical issues.

To overcome this challenge, organizations must invest in continuous training and development for their IT teams. Offering certifications and encouraging employees to attend industry conferences and webinars can help keep the IT staff well-informed about the latest trends and innovations. Collaboration with vendors and staying active in professional networks can also provide valuable insights into emerging technologies.

2. Cybersecurity Concerns

In the digital age, cybersecurity has become one of the most critical aspects of IT support. As businesses store and handle sensitive data and confidential information, protecting against cyber threats is a constant challenge. The ever-evolving nature of cyberattacks makes it difficult for IT teams to anticipate and prevent security breaches effectively.

To address cybersecurity challenges, organizations should implement a robust cybersecurity strategy. This includes regular security audits, threat assessments, and the implementation of security measures such as firewalls, intrusion detection systems, and encryption protocols. Additionally, fostering a culture of security awareness among employees is essential, as they are often the first line of defense against cyber threats.

One of the most significant IT and technical support challenges is finding the right balance between security and user convenience. Strict security measures can sometimes hinder workflow and frustrate users, while lax security can leave the organization vulnerable to cyberattacks.

IT professionals must strike a delicate balance between implementing strong security measures and ensuring a smooth user experience. This requires a deep understanding of the organization's specific needs and risk tolerance. Often, it involves customizing security policies and solutions to match the unique requirements of the business.

Conclusion

IT and technical support challenges are an inherent part of the modern office environment. From addressing technical issues and user complaints to keeping up with rapid technological advancements and enhancing cybersecurity, IT professionals face a multifaceted set of challenges.

To overcome these challenges, organizations should invest in the training and development of their IT teams, provide them with the necessary tools and resources, and foster a culture of continuous improvement. Additionally, striking a balance between security and convenience is crucial, as it ensures that IT support solutions are effective while not hindering the productivity of the workforce.

As technology continues to advance, IT and technical support challenges will persist. However, by acknowledging these challenges and proactively working to address them, businesses can navigate the complex IT landscape more effectively and ensure the smooth functioning of their operations.

Chapter 13. Management and Leadership Challenges

Introduction

In the fast-paced and ever-evolving world of modern business, management and leadership are essential components for the success of any organization. However, with the constantly changing dynamics of the workplace and the diverse needs and aspirations of employees, managers and leaders face a myriad of challenges. This article explores some of the most pressing management and leadership challenges and offers strategies to overcome them. By addressing these challenges, organizations can create a more harmonious and productive work environment, ultimately achieving their goals and objectives.

Balancing Employee Needs and Company Objectives

One of the most significant challenges facing managers and leaders today is striking a balance between the needs of their employees and the objectives of the company. It's a delicate tightrope act that requires a keen understanding of the workforce and the organization's goals. Here's how you can address this challenge:

Empowerment and Autonomy: Encourage employee empowerment and autonomy by allowing them more control over their work. This not only motivates employees but also ensures that individual needs are met, leading to higher job satisfaction and better performance.

Clear Communication: **Open and honest communication is essential. Regularly engage with employees to understand** their concerns, aspirations, and issues. This enables leaders to make informed decisions that align with both employee needs and company objectives.

Flexible Work Arrangements: **Offer flexible work** arrangements, such as remote work or flexible hours, to accommodate various lifestyles and personal circumstances. This demonstrates a commitment to employee well-being and work-life balance while still achieving organizational goals.

Training and Development: Invest in employee training and development. This not only helps employees grow in their careers but also ensures they have the skills and knowledge required to contribute to the company's success.

Recognition and Rewards: Implement a robust recognition and rewards system. Recognizing and rewarding outstanding performance can help motivate employees to align their efforts with company objectives.

Conflict Resolution and Time Management

Conflict resolution and effective time management are two intertwined challenges that leaders and managers encounter regularly. Resolving conflicts efficiently is crucial for maintaining a healthy workplace, while effective time management ensures that objectives are met. Here are some strategies to tackle these challenges:

1. Conflict Resolution

Active Listening: The first step in resolving conflicts is to actively listen to all parties involved. Ensure everyone feels heard and understood.

Mediation: When conflicts persist, consider bringing in a neutral mediator to facilitate a resolution. They can help bridge the communication gap and guide the parties toward a solution.

Conflict Resolution Training: Provide conflict resolution training for employees and managers. This equips individuals with the necessary skills to address and resolve conflicts effectively.

Clear Policies and Procedures: Develop clear conflict resolution policies and procedures within the organization. This establishes a structured framework for addressing disputes and ensures consistency.

2. Time Management

Prioritization: Teach employees and team members how to prioritize tasks. Identifying what is most important and focusing on it is key to effective time management.

Delegation: Managers and leaders should delegate tasks appropriately. Empower team members by entrusting them with tasks that match their skills and capabilities, freeing up time for more critical responsibilities.

Use of Technology: Embrace time management tools and software to streamline work processes. This can include project management software, scheduling tools, and time tracking applications.

Setting Realistic Deadlines: Avoid overloading employees with unrealistic deadlines. Ensure that timeframes for tasks and projects are achievable and consider external factors that may impact timelines.

Conclusion

Management and leadership challenges in the modern workplace are multifaceted, requiring a dynamic approach to address them effectively. Balancing employee needs and company objectives is crucial for fostering a motivated and productive workforce. By empowering employees, ensuring clear communication, offering flexible work arrangements, and recognizing their contributions, leaders can align individual aspirations with the organization's goals.

Conflict resolution and time management are also vital aspects of effective leadership. Addressing conflicts promptly, employing mediation and training, and establishing clear policies can lead to a more harmonious work environment. Simultaneously, effective time management through prioritization, delegation, and technology utilization ensures that both leaders and employees can make the most of their valuable time.

In conclusion, leadership and management challenges are ongoing and ever-evolving. By implementing these strategies and staying attuned to the needs of employees, organizations can overcome these challenges, foster a positive workplace culture, and ultimately achieve their objectives. In a rapidly changing business landscape, adaptability and effective leadership are key to success, allowing companies to navigate challenges and thrive in a competitive world.

Chapter 14. Human Resources Challenges

Introduction

In the fast-paced, ever-evolving world of today's workplaces, human resources (HR) departments face a myriad of challenges. These challenges not only impact the well-being of the employees but also influence the overall productivity and success of an organization. In this article, we will delve into some of the most pressing HR challenges and discuss strategies to overcome them.

Recruitment Challenges

Recruitment is the foundation of any organization's success. Attracting and selecting the right talent is crucial for the overall growth and sustainability of the company. Several key challenges HR professionals encounter during the recruitment process:

Talent Shortages: In an increasingly competitive job market, finding the right candidates for open positions can be challenging. As industries evolve, the demand for specific skills can outpace the availability of qualified professionals.

Strategy: To combat talent shortages, HR departments can invest in training and development programs to upskill existing employees and broaden their talent pool. Partnering with educational institutions and offering internships can also be an effective strategy.

Diversity and Inclusion: A diverse and inclusive workplace is an environment where individuals from various backgrounds, demographics, and perspectives are welcomed, respected, and given equal opportunities. It promotes a sense of belonging and equity, which can lead to improved creativity, innovation, and overall organizational success. Ensuring a diverse and inclusive workplace is not only an ethical imperative but also contributes to a healthier work environment and better business results. HR departments often struggle with promoting diversity in their hiring practices.

Strategy: Employ blind recruitment practices, where personal information such as names and addresses are removed from application materials. Additionally, conducting diversity training and establishing clear diversity goals can help HR teams prioritize diversity and inclusion.

Candidate Experience: Providing a positive candidate experience is essential in attracting top talent. Poor communication, lengthy application processes, and unresponsive HR teams can deter potential candidates.

Strategy: Streamlining the application process, ensuring prompt feedback, and maintaining open communication channels can improve the candidate experience. HR departments should also seek feedback from candidates to continuously enhance their recruitment process.

Talent Retention Challenges

Retaining top talent is as important as recruiting them. High employee turnover can be costly and disruptive. HR professionals must address the following challenges to retain valuable employees:

Competitive Compensation: In a competitive job market, offering attractive compensation packages is crucial. HR departments often face challenges in keeping their compensation strategies up-to-date.

Strategy: Conduct regular market salary research to ensure that your compensation packages remain competitive. Consider performance-based bonuses, stock options, and other non-monetary benefits to attract and retain talent.

Stock options refer to a form of compensation offered to employees, typically at a specific price (the "strike price"), that allows them to purchase a certain number of company shares at a future date. These options can be part of an employee's overall compensation package and are often used as an incentive for them to contribute to the company's growth and success, as they may profit from any increase in the company's stock price when they exercise their options.

Work-Life Balance: In today's fast-paced work environments, maintaining a healthy work-life balance can be challenging for employees. HR must create an environment that encourages employees to maintain a balance between their professional and personal lives.

Strategy: Offer flexible working arrangements, such as remote work options or flexible hours, to promote work-life balance. Encourage employees to take time off when needed and prioritize mental health and well-being.

Career Development: Employees often leave organizations due to a perceived lack of opportunities for career growth. HR must provide pathways for professional development and growth within the company.

Strategy: Create a structured career development program that includes mentoring, training, and opportunities for advancement within the organization. Encourage employees to set and work towards career goals.

Conflict Resolution Challenges

Conflict is a natural part of any workplace, but HR professionals are tasked with managing and resolving these issues to maintain a harmonious work environment. Common challenges include:

Communication Breakdown: Miscommunication and misunderstandings among employees can escalate into conflicts. HR must address these issues promptly to prevent further discord.

Strategy: Implement effective communication training for all employees to improve their interpersonal skills. Additionally, establish a clear and confidential process for reporting conflicts, with HR serving as a neutral mediator.

Personality Clashes: Differences in personality and working styles can lead to conflicts among team members. HR professionals often struggle to resolve these clashes.

Strategy: Encourage team-building activities and assessments that help employees better understand each other's strengths and weaknesses. Provide conflict resolution training for managers and employees to address and manage interpersonal conflicts more effectively.

Unresolved Issues: In some cases, conflicts are left unresolved or ignored, leading to increased tension and workplace toxicity.

Strategy: Create a conflict resolution framework that includes clear procedures for identifying, addressing, and resolving conflicts. Encourage open dialogue and provide resources for mediation when necessary.

Legal Compliance Challenges

Labor laws and regulations are legal guidelines that govern the rights, duties, and working conditions of employees and employers. Staying compliant with labor laws and regulations is a fundamental HR responsibility. Non-compliance can lead to costly legal issues and reputational damage. Common legal compliance challenges include:

Changing Regulations: Labor laws and regulations are subject to frequent changes. HR professionals must stay updated and ensure that their organization complies with the latest legal requirements.

Strategy: Invest in continuous training for HR staff to keep them informed about legal updates and changes. Establish a compliance team responsible for monitoring and implementing necessary changes in policies and procedures.

Data Privacy: As data becomes increasingly integral to HR functions, maintaining data privacy and security is a top concern. Ensuring that employee data is handled in accordance with relevant laws is challenging.

Strategy: Develop and implement strict data protection policies and procedures. Regularly audit data handling practices and provide training on data privacy to all employees.

Workplace Harassment and Discrimination: Preventing and addressing workplace harassment and discrimination is a critical legal and ethical responsibility for HR.

 Implement strict anti-harassment and discrimination policies, along with training programs to educate employees and management. Ensure that reporting procedures are confidential and that complaints are thoroughly investigated and addressed.

Conclusion

In the ever-evolving world of work, human resources departments face a wide range of challenges. Recruitment and talent retention are critical to an organization's success, and HR professionals must continually adapt to overcome challenges such as talent shortages, diversity and inclusion, and improving the candidate experience. Employee conflicts can disrupt the workplace, and HR's role in resolving them is essential. Effective communication, conflict resolution, and mediation strategies are vital for maintaining a harmonious work environment. Additionally, legal compliance is non-negotiable, and HR departments must continually adapt to changing regulations, maintain data privacy, and address workplace harassment and discrimination.

By acknowledging and addressing these challenges, HR professionals can play a pivotal role in shaping a positive and productive workplace, ultimately contributing to the long-term success of their organizations. In doing so, they will not only overcome office challenges but also pave the way for a more engaged and satisfied workforce, fostering a culture of growth and prosperity.

Chapter 15. Finance and Accounting Challenges

Introduction

In the fast-paced world of business, finance and accounting are two pillars that provide the stability and direction needed for an organization's success. However, these departments are not immune to challenges. In fact, they often face a multitude of obstacles that can impede their effectiveness. From managing budgets and financial reporting to reducing financial inefficiencies and ensuring tax compliance, finance and accounting professionals navigate a complex landscape. In this article, we will explore these common finance and accounting challenges and discuss effective strategies to overcome them. By addressing these issues head-on, organizations can ensure their financial departments are running smoothly, contributing to overall success.

Managing Budgets and Financial Reporting

Effective budget management is a cornerstone of financial stability for any organization. Budgets help allocate resources, set financial goals, and monitor progress. However, several challenges are commonly associated with managing budgets and financial reporting.

Changing Market Conditions: The ever-evolving business landscape means that budgets often need to be adjusted to accommodate changes in market conditions, which can be challenging to predict or respond to effectively.

Strategy: Implement rolling budgets that allow for continuous updates and revisions. This approach ensures budgets remain adaptable and responsive to market fluctuations.

Data Accuracy and Integrity: Financial reporting relies heavily on accurate data. Errors or inconsistencies in data can lead to incorrect financial statements and decision-making.

Strategy: Invest in robust accounting software that automates data entry and reconciliation, reducing the risk of human errors. Implement rigorous data validation procedures to maintain data integrity.

Complex Regulatory Compliance: Navigating the ever-changing landscape of financial regulations and compliance requirements can be a daunting task for finance and accounting teams.

Strategy: Stay updated with the latest regulations and compliance requirements by working closely with legal and regulatory experts. Implement automated compliance monitoring and reporting tools to ensure adherence to changing laws.

Lack of Visibility: In larger organizations, various departments often create their budgets and financial reports in isolation. This lack of visibility can lead to inefficiencies and redundancies.

Strategy: Establish cross-functional teams that collaborate to develop budgets and financial reports, fostering transparency and streamlining processes.

Inadequate Reporting Tools: Outdated or inefficient reporting tools can hinder the generation of meaningful financial reports.

Strategy: Invest in modern financial reporting software that provides real-time data analysis and visualization, making it easier to generate comprehensive, accurate reports.

Reducing Financial Inefficiencies and Tax Compliance

Financial inefficiencies can lead to substantial losses and hinder an organization's growth. Additionally, tax compliance is a critical aspect of financial management that cannot be overlooked. Addressing these challenges is crucial for maintaining financial health and regulatory adherence.

Inefficient Manual Processes: Reliance on manual data entry and processing can lead to inefficiencies, errors, and wasted time.

Strategy: Automate repetitive and time-consuming processes, such as invoice processing and payroll, to reduce errors and increase efficiency.

Inadequate Cash Flow Management: Poor cash flow management can result in cash shortages, leading to financial instability.

Strategy: Implement cash flow forecasting tools to predict and manage cash needs more effectively. Create a cash flow policy that defines when and how funds are disbursed and received.

Tax Compliance Challenges: Ensuring tax compliance is a complex task, as tax laws and regulations frequently change.

Strategy: Partner with a tax expert or firm to stay updated on tax laws. Implement tax compliance software to help automate tax-related tasks and ensure accurate filing.

Inefficient Expense Tracking: Poor tracking of expenses can lead to overspending and a lack of control over financial resources.

Strategy: Use expense management software to track and analyze expenses in real-time. Implement a clear expense policy that outlines permissible expenses and their limits.

Data Security Concerns: Financial data is sensitive and must be protected from cyber threats and data breaches.

Strategy: Invest in robust data security measures, including encryption, access controls, and regular security audits. Provide employee training on data security best practices.

Conclusion

Finance and accounting are the backbone of any organization, and addressing the challenges faced by these departments is crucial for business success. From managing budgets and financial reporting to reducing inefficiencies and ensuring tax compliance, there are numerous obstacles that must be overcome.

To navigate the ever-changing financial landscape effectively, organizations must adapt and implement strategies tailored to their specific challenges. The strategies discussed in this article provide a foundation for addressing common finance and accounting challenges, but it's essential for organizations to continually evaluate and fine-tune their approaches based on their unique needs.

In conclusion, by proactively addressing these challenges, organizations can strengthen their financial departments and enhance their overall financial stability. The ability to manage budgets effectively, produce accurate financial reports, reduce inefficiencies, and maintain tax compliance is not only essential for compliance with legal and regulatory requirements but also for achieving long-term financial success.

To overcome these challenges, organizations must be willing to invest in technology, training, and the expertise required to ensure the financial and accounting functions are operating at their best. In doing so, they can reap the rewards of a well-managed financial department, which will contribute to the overall success and sustainability of the organization.

Introduction

Effective communication is the cornerstone of a successful and harmonious workplace. In today's fast-paced business environment, where teams often comprise diverse individuals with varying personalities, communication plays a pivotal role in ensuring productivity and resolving challenges. In this article, we'll explore how effective communication in the office can address issues such as conflict resolution, office politics, time management, and work-life balance, ultimately contributing to a more efficient and enjoyable work environment.

Effective communication is the lifeblood of any organization. It is not just about conveying information but about understanding and being understood. The office, being a dynamic and complex environment, presents unique challenges that require strategic communication to navigate. Without effective communication, these challenges can turn into major hurdles, impeding productivity, and causing stress among employees.

In this article, we will discuss how effective communication can be employed to address several common office challenges.

Conflict Resolution and Office Politics

1. Recognizing the Signs of Conflict

Conflict is an inevitable part of any workplace. It can stem from differences in opinions, misunderstandings, or competition for limited resources. However, it's how conflicts are handled that can make or break a team's cohesion.

Recognizing the early signs of conflict is crucial. Effective communication involves paying attention to subtle cues like increased tension, passive-aggressive behavior, or a decline in team collaboration. *Passive-aggressive behavior* is a pattern of expressing negative feelings or resistance indirectly, often through subtle acts of defiance, non-cooperation, or disguised hostility rather than through open communication. By identifying these signs, you can intervene before the conflict escalates.

2. Open and Honest Communication

When conflict arises, it's essential to foster an environment where open and honest communication is encouraged. Encourage team members to express their concerns, feelings, and viewpoints in a safe and respectful manner.

Active listening is equally crucial in conflict resolution. It ensures that all parties involved feel heard and understood. By actively listening to the perspectives of all those involved, you can start to build a bridge towards resolution.

3. Mediation and Collaboration

In more severe cases of conflict, mediation may be necessary. A neutral third party, often a manager or HR professional, can help facilitate communication between the conflicting parties. They can identify common ground and encourage compromise.

Additionally, promoting collaboration rather than competition within the office can prevent many conflicts from arising. By fostering a team spirit, encouraging the sharing of ideas, and recognizing individual contributions, you can minimize the opportunities for conflict to take root.

Time Management and Work-Life Balance

1. Setting Clear Expectations

In the modern office, time is a precious resource, and effective time management is vital for both personal and organizational success. Employees often struggle with managing their time, leading to stress, missed deadlines, and a lack of work-life balance.

One aspect of effective communication is setting clear expectations. Managers should communicate project deadlines, priorities, and responsibilities to their teams. When everyone is on the same page, it's easier to allocate time effectively.

2. Prioritization and Delegation

To enhance time management, employees need to learn how to prioritize their tasks. This involves understanding which tasks are urgent, important, or can be deferred. Effective communication allows team members to collaborate and delegate tasks based on individual strengths and availability.

Managers should also communicate their expectations regarding the delegation of tasks. This can help prevent misunderstandings and ensure that everyone's workload is manageable.

3. Open Dialogue on Work-Life Balance

The concept of work-life balance is closely related to time management. It's about ensuring that employees have the time and energy to lead fulfilling personal lives while excelling at their jobs.

Managers should promote an open dialogue about work-life balance. This includes encouraging employees to voice their concerns, express their needs, and request flexibility when necessary. When employees feel that their needs are heard and accommodated, they are more likely to be satisfied and productive.

Office Politics

1. Transparency and Fairness

Office politics can often disrupt the harmony of a workplace. It typically involves individuals pursuing personal interests or power at the expense of others. Effective communication can help reduce the negative impact of office politics.

Promoting transparency and fairness is key. When employees feel that decisions are made openly and impartially, it reduces the scope for underhanded politics. Managers should communicate their commitment to these values and be consistent in their application.

2. Encourage Constructive Feedback

Open channels for constructive feedback can serve as a release valve for office politics. Employees should feel free to express their concerns and opinions about office dynamics without fear of retribution.

Effective communication involves creating feedback mechanisms, such as regular team meetings, anonymous suggestion boxes, or one-on-one discussions. This allows employees to express their concerns and insights, contributing to a healthier work environment.

3. Leadership by Example

Managers play a crucial role in shaping the office culture. They need to lead by example, demonstrating ethical behavior, and communicating the values of integrity, respect, and teamwork.

When leaders uphold these principles and communicate them to their teams, it sets the tone for the entire organization. Employees are more likely to follow suit and engage in positive interactions, reducing the prevalence of negative office politics.

Conclusion

In the dynamic and fast-paced world of the modern office, effective communication is the bedrock of overcoming the many challenges that arise. Whether dealing with conflict, office politics, time management, or work-life balance, communication serves as the solution. By recognizing the signs of conflict, promoting open and honest communication, and fostering collaboration, we can navigate through turbulent waters and reach amicable resolutions.

To improve time management and work-life balance, setting clear expectations, prioritization, delegation, and encouraging open dialogues on work-life balance are key strategies. Ensuring that employees can voice their concerns and request flexibility empowers them to achieve a healthier balance.

Finally, to tackle the pervasive issue of office politics, promoting transparency and fairness, encouraging constructive feedback, and demonstrating ethical leadership by example can reshape office culture and mitigate the negative impact of politics.

Incorporating these strategies into your office environment can pave the way for a more harmonious, productive, and satisfying workplace. Effective communication is the linchpin that holds everything together, ensuring that teams can work cohesively and overcome the multifaceted challenges of the modern office.

Introduction

In today's fast-paced and constantly evolving business landscape, office technology and innovation have become indispensable tools for organizations striving to overcome the numerous challenges they face daily. The modern office is no longer confined to brick-and-mortar walls; it's an intricate ecosystem where technology seamlessly interweaves with daily operations, transforming the way we work and addressing a myriad of office challenges. This article explores the dynamic relationship between office technology and innovation, demonstrating how they provide innovative solutions to enhance office efficiency and ultimately overcome the challenges that businesses encounter in their pursuit of success.

The Impact of Technology on Office Challenges

1. Streamlining Communication

One of the fundamental challenges faced by offices is the efficient communication of information. In the past, inter-office communication often relied on physical documents, memos, and in-person meetings, which were time-consuming and prone to errors. However, technology has revolutionized the way offices communicate. The advent of email, instant messaging platforms, and video conferencing tools has enabled real-time, seamless, and global communication. Employees can now connect instantly, making remote work and collaboration more efficient than ever.

2. Increasing Productivity

Workplace productivity is a crucial aspect of office operations. Technology has introduced various tools and software applications that empower employees to work smarter, not harder. Project management software, for instance, helps teams organize tasks and deadlines effectively, while automation tools eliminate repetitive tasks, allowing employees to focus on more strategic work. In addition, the rise of cloud computing enables employees to access documents and data from anywhere, enhancing flexibility and productivity.

3. Enhancing Data Management

Managing and storing data is a significant challenge for offices, particularly in a digital era where data is generated at an unprecedented rate. Technological innovations have addressed this issue through data storage solutions like cloud services, which not only offer secure storage but also facilitate easy sharing and access. Additionally, the integration of artificial intelligence (AI) and machine learning in data management helps organizations derive valuable insights from their data, guiding informed decision-making.

4. Employee Engagement and Satisfaction

In an age where attracting and retaining top talent is highly competitive, technology has played a pivotal role in enhancing employee engagement and satisfaction. Remote work options, flexible scheduling, and wellness apps have improved the work-life balance, promoting a happier and more productive workforce. Collaborative tools have also contributed to a sense of belonging and connection, even in virtual work environments. *Collaborative tools* are software and applications that facilitate communication, coordination, and teamwork among individuals and groups, allowing them to work together on projects, share information, and achieve common goals, often in a digital or remote environment.

5. Cybersecurity Challenges

The digital transformation has brought about an array of security concerns. Cyberattacks, data breaches, and privacy threats are real challenges that modern offices face. Innovative solutions like advanced encryption, multi-factor authentication, and cybersecurity training programs are vital in safeguarding sensitive data and protecting the organization from potential cyber threats.

Innovative Solutions for Office Efficiency

1. Automation and AI

One of the most significant innovations in modern offices is the integration of automation and artificial intelligence. Automation has streamlined repetitive tasks, reducing the margin of human error and allowing employees to focus on more complex, creative, and value-added work. AI-driven algorithms and machine learning models analyze vast datasets to offer insights, predictions, and recommendations, which inform strategic decisions. For instance, customer service chatbots have revolutionized customer support, offering quick and efficient responses to customer inquiries.

2. Cloud Computing

Cloud computing solutions have provided offices with a flexible and scalable platform for data storage, sharing, and application hosting. The cloud has reduced the need for costly on-premises servers and hardware, allowing organizations to scale their resources according to their needs. Additionally, it enables remote access to data and applications, fostering a more flexible work environment, particularly in today's era of remote work.

3. Remote Work Technology

The global COVID-19 pandemic catapulted remote work into the spotlight, necessitating advanced remote work technology solutions. Video conferencing tools like Zoom and Microsoft Teams, collaboration platforms like Slack and Trello, and virtual private network (VPN) services have become integral for maintaining productivity and communication in remote work settings. These tools have facilitated team collaboration, even when employees are dispersed across different locations.

4. Internet of Things (IoT)

The Internet of Things (IoT) has revolutionized office operations by connecting everyday devices to the internet. Smart offices utilize IoT to optimize energy consumption, monitor office equipment, and enhance security through connected sensors and devices. This not only reduces operational costs but also enhances employee comfort and safety.

5. Data Analytics

Data analytics tools are transforming the way offices make decisions. By extracting valuable insights from large datasets, businesses can make informed, data-driven decisions to drive growth. Analytics tools help identify trends, patterns, and correlations, allowing businesses to adjust their strategies, marketing efforts, and operations to meet market demands effectively.

6. Cybersecurity Solutions

As cyber threats evolve, so do the solutions to combat them. Offices now employ advanced cybersecurity solutions such as next-generation firewalls, intrusion detection systems, and artificial intelligence-based threat detection. Regular employee training on cybersecurity best practices is also crucial in creating a culture of security awareness within the organization.

Conclusion

Office technology and innovation are inseparable allies in the quest to overcome the diverse challenges faced by modern workplaces. From streamlining communication to enhancing productivity, the impact of technology on offices is profound. Innovative solutions have revolutionized how offices operate, improving efficiency and addressing long-standing challenges.

As we move forward, embracing these technological advancements and staying attuned to the ever-evolving landscape of innovation will be vital for offices seeking a competitive edge. The future promises even more exciting developments, such as augmented reality (AR), virtual reality (VR), and blockchain, which have the potential to further transform the way we work.

In conclusion, offices must continue to adapt to the dynamic intersection of technology and innovation, recognizing that these tools are essential for navigating the challenges of the modern business world. By doing so, businesses can position themselves for success, not only overcoming current challenges but also preparing for the ones that lie ahead in an ever-changing landscape. Office technology and innovation are not merely assets; they are the keys to thriving in a future that is constantly evolving.

Chapter 18. Employee Engagement and Company Culture

Introduction

Employee engagement refers to the emotional commitment and dedication that employees have towards their work and their organization. *Company culture* encompasses the values, beliefs, norms, and behaviors that define the work environment and the way employees interact with one another and the organization.

In the modern workplace, where competition is fierce and talent is at a premium, companies are increasingly recognizing the importance of employee engagement and company culture as key drivers of success. The concept of a positive company culture and engaged employees has gained significant traction in recent years, and for a good reason. A workplace that fosters engagement and cultivates a strong culture can lead to increased productivity, higher employee retention, and a more enjoyable work environment.

In this article, we will delve into the critical components of employee engagement and company culture, exploring the strategies that can help organizations overcome common office challenges. From creating a positive company culture to keeping employees engaged and motivated, we will discuss how these elements are intrinsically connected and contribute to a thriving workplace.

Creating a Positive Company Culture

A positive company culture is the foundation upon which a productive and engaging work environment is built. It encompasses the values, beliefs, behaviors, and attitudes that define a company and its employees. A strong company culture provides a sense of purpose and belonging, making employees more likely to invest themselves in their work. Here are some strategies for cultivating a positive company culture:

Define and Communicate Core Values: To establish a positive company culture, it's essential to define the organization's core values. These values should guide decision-making and behaviors at all levels of the company. Once these values are established, it is crucial to communicate them clearly and consistently to all employees.

Lead by Example: Leadership sets the tone for the entire organization. When leaders consistently embody the company's values, it creates a powerful example for others to follow. Leaders should not only articulate the values but also live them in their daily interactions.

Empower Employees: A positive culture values employees' input and contributions. Empower employees to have a say in decision-making processes, and encourage them to take ownership of their work. This not only fosters a sense of belonging but also motivates individuals to work towards the company's goals.

Recognition and Appreciation: Recognizing and appreciating employees for their hard work and achievements is an integral part of a positive culture. Acknowledgment can come in various forms, from verbal praise to rewards and incentives. A culture of recognition fosters a sense of accomplishment and motivation.

Diversity and Inclusion: Embracing diversity and promoting inclusion are essential elements of a positive company culture. A diverse workforce brings a variety of perspectives, fostering creativity and innovation. Inclusion ensures that every employee feels valued and has equal opportunities.

Continuous Learning: Encourage a culture of continuous learning and development. Provide opportunities for skill enhancement and personal growth. When employees feel that the company invests in their development, they are more likely to engage and remain committed.

Keeping Employees Engaged and Motivated

Employee engagement is the emotional commitment an employee has towards their organization. Engaged employees are enthusiastic about their work, feel connected to the company's mission, and actively contribute to its success. When employees are engaged, they are not only more productive but also less likely to seek opportunities elsewhere. Here are some strategies to keep employees engaged and motivated:

Clear Expectations: Employees need to know what is expected of them. Clear job descriptions, well-defined roles, and performance expectations help reduce ambiguity and anxiety. When employees understand their responsibilities, they can focus on meeting and exceeding them.

Feedback and Performance Reviews: Regular feedback and performance reviews are vital for employee development.

Constructive feedback helps employees understand their strengths and areas for improvement. It also provides a platform for discussing goals and career growth.

Career Path Development: Offering a clear career path within the organization can significantly boost employee engagement. When employees see opportunities for advancement and personal growth, they are more likely to remain committed to their jobs.

Work-Life Balance: Striking a healthy work-life balance is essential for employee well-being. Encourage employees to take breaks, use their vacation days, and maintain boundaries between work and personal life. A burnt-out employee is unlikely to be engaged or productive.

Flexibility and Autonomy: Granting employees a degree of flexibility and autonomy in their work can be a powerful motivator. It allows them to take ownership of their tasks and work in a way that suits their strengths and preferences.

Team Building and Collaboration: Building a sense of community and teamwork is crucial for engagement. Encourage collaboration and team-building activities to strengthen bonds among employees. A cohesive team is more likely to be engaged and motivated.

Incentives and Rewards: Incentives and rewards, such as bonuses, promotions, and recognition, can provide strong motivation. Employees who see tangible rewards for their hard work are more likely to remain engaged and committed.

Wellness Programs: Promote employee wellness through programs that address physical and mental health. A healthy employee is more likely to be engaged and productive. Provide resources and support to help employees maintain their well-being.

Conclusion

In the competitive landscape of today's business world, companies are faced with numerous challenges. Yet, a strong company culture and engaged employees can help organizations not only survive but thrive. The strategies discussed in this article underscore the importance of fostering a positive company culture and keeping employees engaged and motivated.

By defining and communicating core values, leading by example, empowering employees, and promoting diversity and inclusion, companies can create a culture that employees will want to be a part of. This culture, in turn, contributes to employee engagement by providing a sense of purpose and belonging.

To keep employees engaged and motivated, organizations should ensure clear expectations, provide regular feedback, offer opportunities for career growth, promote work-life balance, and encourage flexibility. Team building, incentives, and wellness programs further contribute to employee well-being and engagement.

In conclusion, overcoming office challenges is not just about addressing external factors but also about nurturing the internal elements of a company. A positive company culture and engaged employees are integral to a successful organization. By implementing the strategies discussed in this article, companies can create a workplace where employees are not just motivated but genuinely invested in the company's success, thereby ensuring their own growth and prosperity.

Introduction

The modern office is a dynamic, ever-evolving environment. It's no longer the static, cubicle-filled space it used to be. Today, offices are adaptive and responsive, constantly changing to meet the demands of a rapidly shifting world. As we enter an era where technology, demographics, and the very nature of work are in flux, adaptability in the workplace has become a vital skill.

In this article, we'll explore the need for adaptability in the modern office and discuss strategies for thriving amidst change. The modern office, in all its complexities, presents a multitude of challenges that can be overcome with the right mindset and approach.

The Need for Adaptability in the Workplace

1. Technological Advancements

One of the most significant drivers of change in the modern office is technological advancement. New tools, software, and devices emerge almost daily, altering the way we work and communicate. To stay relevant, employees and organizations alike must continually update their skill sets and systems. For instance, the adoption of cloud-based collaboration platforms, remote work tools, and AI-powered processes has reshaped the way businesses function.

In this context, employees who resist change are at risk of becoming outdated and inefficient. As technology evolves, those who are adaptable and eager to learn are more likely to thrive in the modern office. Continuous training and upskilling are essential to remain relevant in a tech-driven world.

2. Remote and Hybrid Work Models

The COVID-19 pandemic accelerated a trend that was already gaining momentum: remote work. With the rapid shift to telecommuting, organizations had to adapt quickly to support remote employees and manage remote teams. This change required not only technological adjustments but also a shift in mindset. Managers had to learn how to lead remote teams effectively, and employees had to develop new ways of working independently.

As the pandemic subsides, many organizations have adopted hybrid work models, combining in-office and remote work. This creates new challenges in terms of coordination, communication, and maintaining a sense of belonging among team members. Adapting to these evolving work models is vital for both employers and employees.

3. Diverse and Inclusive Workplaces

Diversity and inclusion are not just buzzwords in the modern office; they are integral to success. A diverse workforce brings different perspectives, ideas, and problem-solving approaches to the table. However, adapting to a diverse workplace requires openness, cultural competence, and the ability to communicate and collaborate effectively with individuals from various backgrounds.

To foster a truly inclusive work environment, organizations must provide training, education, and resources to help employees adapt to and celebrate diversity. Leaders need to model inclusive behavior, and employees should actively engage in creating an inclusive culture.

4. Shifting Employee Expectations

Millennials (born between the early 1980s and the mid-1990s) and Generation Z (born from the mid-1990s to the early 2010s) have entered the workforce with different expectations than previous generations. They value work-life balance, purpose-driven work, and opportunities for continuous learning and development. This shift in employee expectations has forced organizations to rethink their traditional structures and policies.

To attract and retain top talent, companies must adapt by offering flexible work arrangements, mentorship programs, and opportunities for growth. As a result, the modern office is becoming more accommodating to the needs and desires of younger generations.

Strategies to Overcome Office Challenges

1. Embrace Lifelong Learning

Adaptability starts with a commitment to lifelong learning. Employees must take ownership of their professional development, seeking out opportunities to acquire new skills and knowledge. Employers, in turn, should provide resources for training and encourage employees to explore and experiment.

Continuous learning can take various forms, from online courses and workshops to mentoring and cross-training programs. It's a proactive approach to staying relevant in a rapidly changing workplace. Those who embrace lifelong learning are more likely to adapt seamlessly to new technologies and work processes.

2. Develop Resilience

Resilience is the ability to bounce back from setbacks and adapt to adversity. In the modern office, challenges and change are inevitable. Therefore, developing resilience is essential for both individuals and organizations.

To enhance resilience, employees can practice stress management techniques, maintain a healthy work-life balance, and seek support from peers and mentors. Organizations can create a culture of psychological safety where employees feel comfortable acknowledging challenges and seeking assistance. This fosters an environment where people are more willing to adapt and overcome obstacles.

3. Cultivate Strong Communication Skills

Adaptability is closely tied to effective communication. As the modern office becomes more collaborative and diverse, the ability to communicate across various channels and with people from different backgrounds is crucial.

To enhance communication skills, employees can engage in workshops or training programs that focus on active listening, conflict resolution, and intercultural communication. For organizations, it's essential to establish clear communication protocols and provide tools that facilitate effective collaboration.

4. Foster a Growth Mindset

A growth mindset is the belief that abilities and intelligence can be developed through effort and learning. People with a growth mindset are more likely to embrace challenges and see failures as opportunities for growth. In contrast, those with a fixed mindset may resist change and be less adaptable.

Leaders can promote a growth mindset by encouraging risk-taking, recognizing and rewarding effort, and creating an atmosphere where employees feel comfortable taking on new challenges. This mindset shift can lead to a more adaptable and innovative workplace.

5. Embrace Agile Work Practices

Agile work practices involve flexible, collaborative, and iterative approaches to project management, emphasizing adaptability and efficiency. Agile methodologies, originally designed for software development, have found their way into various aspects of business, from project management to organizational culture. The agile approach emphasizes adaptability, collaboration, and iterative progress.

Agile work practices can be applied to tasks beyond software development. Teams can use agile principles to manage projects, make strategic decisions, and adapt to changing market conditions. By embracing agile practices, organizations become more resilient and better equipped to navigate the uncertainties of the modern office.

Conclusion

Adapting to change in the modern office is no longer an optional skill; it's a necessity for individuals and organizations. The workplace of today is marked by rapid technological advancements, evolving work models, diverse and inclusive cultures, and shifting employee expectations. In the face of these challenges, the ability to adapt and thrive is what sets successful individuals and organizations apart.

To succeed in this dynamic environment, individuals should prioritize lifelong learning, develop resilience, cultivate strong communication skills, foster a growth mindset, and embrace agile work practices. These strategies will not only help employees navigate change but also contribute to a culture of adaptability within organizations.

In the end, adaptability is the cornerstone of resilience and innovation. Those who are willing to embrace change will find themselves better equipped to face the challenges and opportunities that the modern office presents. As we continue to witness the transformation of the workplace, adaptability remains the key to thriving in this ever-changing landscape.

Introduction

In today's fast-paced business environment, office challenges are ubiquitous. While many of these challenges are operational or interpersonal in nature, legal challenges often loom as significant threats to the smooth functioning of any office. These legal challenges encompass a wide range of issues, from compliance with labor laws to data security and cybersecurity concerns. In this article, we will explore some of the most prominent legal challenges faced by modern offices and discuss strategies to overcome them.

Addressing Legal Issues and Compliance

1. Labor Laws and Employment Compliance

One of the most critical legal challenges for any office is ensuring compliance with labor laws and employment regulations. Laws and regulations regarding wages, working hours, discrimination, harassment, and workplace safety can vary significantly from one jurisdiction to another. Failure to comply with these regulations can result in lawsuits, fines, and damage to a company's reputation.

To address this challenge, offices should:

- Stay informed about local, state, and federal labor laws.
- Regularly review and update employment policies and procedures to ensure compliance.
- Provide training for employees and managers on issues such as discrimination and harassment prevention.

❖ Establish open channels of communication to allow employees to report any violations or concerns.

2. Intellectual Property Protection

Offices that deal with creative work, intellectual property, or proprietary technology must safeguard their intellectual property rights. Unauthorized use, theft, or infringement of intellectual property can lead to costly legal battles.

To protect intellectual property, offices can:

❖ Implement confidentiality agreements and non-disclosure agreements (NDAs) with employees and contractors.
❖ Register trademarks, copyrights, and patents when applicable.
❖ Educate employees about the importance of protecting intellectual property.
❖ Monitor for potential infringements and take prompt legal action when necessary.

3. Contractual Agreements and Disputes

Offices often rely on contracts to establish legal relationships with clients, vendors, and partners. Disputes related to contractual agreements can be time-consuming and costly. To mitigate the risk of disputes:

❖ Ensure that contracts are drafted clearly and unambiguously.
❖ Review contracts carefully and seek legal counsel when necessary.
❖ Establish dispute resolution mechanisms, such as arbitration or mediation, in contracts to expedite conflict resolution.

Data Security and Cybersecurity

1. Data Privacy and Compliance

With the increasing reliance on digital technologies, data privacy and compliance have become paramount legal challenges for offices. Regulations like the General Data Protection Regulation (GDPR) in Europe and the California Consumer Privacy Act (CCPA) in the United States impose strict requirements on how personal data is collected, processed, and protected.

To navigate data privacy challenges:

- ❖ Understand and comply with relevant data protection regulations.
- ❖ Appoint a data protection officer if necessary.
- ❖ Implement robust data security measures, such as encryption and access controls.
- ❖ Conduct regular audits to ensure compliance and data protection.

2. Cybersecurity Threats

The rise of cyberattacks and data breaches poses a significant legal challenge to offices. Breaches can result in legal repercussions, fines, and damage to a company's reputation. Offices must proactively address this threat.

- ❖ Develop a comprehensive cybersecurity policy that includes employee training on security best practices.
- ❖ Invest in advanced cybersecurity technologies and regularly update them.

❖ Perform regular security assessments and penetration testing to identify vulnerabilities.
❖ Develop an incident response plan to manage and mitigate the impact of cyberattacks.

3. Employee Data Protection

As offices collect and store employee data, they must ensure the protection of sensitive information, such as social security numbers, medical records, and financial data. Failing to safeguard employee data can lead to legal consequences.

To protect employee data:

❖ Limit access to sensitive information to only authorized personnel.
❖ Encrypt employee data during transmission and storage.
❖ Regularly audit data handling practices to identify and rectify vulnerabilities.
❖ Provide employees with information about how their data is used and protected.

Conclusion

Legal challenges in the office are a complex and ever-evolving landscape. Offices must be proactive in addressing these challenges to avoid costly legal battles, fines, and reputational damage. Staying informed about labor laws and employment compliance, safeguarding intellectual property, and addressing contractual disputes are crucial aspects of navigating the legal landscape.

In the digital age, data security and cybersecurity concerns add another layer of complexity to legal challenges. Offices must adhere to data protection regulations, implement robust cybersecurity measures, and protect employee data to avoid legal consequences and data breaches.

As the legal landscape continues to evolve, offices must remain vigilant, adapt to changing regulations, and prioritize compliance and data protection. By addressing these legal challenges head-on, offices can reduce their exposure to legal risks and focus on their core mission of productivity and growth.

As we bring our journey through the various challenges and strategies in the modern office to a close, we find ourselves at the crossroads of a shifting landscape. The future of office work is a dynamic terrain, shaped by ever-evolving technology, changing workplace dynamics, and the ongoing quest for employee well-being and productivity. In this final chapter of "Strategies to Overcome Office Challenges," we reflect on the key takeaways and anticipate the trajectory of office work in the years to come.

Key Takeaways

Our exploration of office challenges and strategies has illuminated several key takeaways that serve as pillars for the future of work.

Embracing Technology: Technological disruptions are inevitable, and embracing them rather than resisting is key to staying competitive. Automation, artificial intelligence, and remote work tools will continue to play a significant role in reshaping office work.

Interpersonal Dynamics: Building and maintaining harmonious workplace relationships is crucial. Effective communication, conflict resolution, and empathy are essential for a positive workplace environment.

Time Management: Mastery of time management is vital. Productivity tools and techniques will become increasingly important as work becomes more complex and interconnected.

Well-being: Recognizing and addressing stress and burnout signs is vital for employee well-being. Strategies to promote mental and physical health are indispensable in the office.

Self-Management: Taking control of one's work life is empowering. Self-discipline, organization, and personal development will be essential skills for employees.

Leadership's Role: Effective leadership plays a pivotal role in overcoming office challenges. Leaders must adapt to changing workplace dynamics and be responsive to their teams' needs.

Common Challenges Across Roles: While specific roles have unique challenges, there are common threads that tie all office workers together. These include effective communication, adaptability, and problem-solving skills.

Role-Specific Challenges: Understanding the unique challenges in various roles, such as sales and marketing, IT, management, human resources, finance, and accounting, is key to providing targeted solutions.

Office Culture and Employee Engagement: A positive company culture and high employee engagement are essential for a thriving workplace. Cultivating a sense of belonging and purpose will be an enduring focus.

Adapting to Change: In the rapidly evolving modern office, adaptability is a must. Being open to change and continuously learning will define the successful employees of the future.

Legal Considerations: As regulations and compliance requirements evolve, staying informed about legal challenges is crucial for protecting both the organization and its employees.

The Evolving Landscape of Office Work

To envision the future of office work, we must recognize the ongoing trends and transformations that are shaping it. These trends are interwoven and reflect the complex and multifaceted nature of work in the 21st century.

Remote Work: The COVID-19 pandemic accelerated the adoption of remote work. While it may not become the exclusive norm, hybrid work arrangements will persist. This necessitates a reimagining of office spaces and a more flexible approach to work.

Automation and AI: The integration of automation and artificial intelligence is not about replacing jobs but enhancing them. Routine tasks will be automated, allowing employees to focus on creativity, problem-solving, and strategic thinking.

Flexible Scheduling: Work-life balance is at the forefront of employee demands. Flexible scheduling and alternative work arrangements will become more common, promoting well-being and reducing burnout.

Diversity and Inclusion: Diversity, equity, and inclusion are not just buzzwords. They are integral to a healthy workplace culture. Companies that invest in diversity and inclusion will be better positioned to attract and retain top talent.

Sustainability: The corporate world is increasingly aware of its environmental impact. Sustainable practices and environmentally friendly policies will shape the office of the future.

Reskilling and Upskilling: **The pace of change demands continuous learning. Employers and employees must invest in reskilling and upskilling to stay competitive in the job market.**

Well-being Initiatives: **Mental and physical health will be at the forefront of workplace initiatives. Companies will prioritize well-being to enhance employee morale and productivity.**

Evolving Leadership Styles: **Leadership styles will adapt to a more decentralized, collaborative, and empathetic model. The traditional hierarchical structure may evolve to one that is more agile and responsive.**

Conclusion

The future of office work is characterized by adaptability, technology integration, and a focus on holistic employee well-being. It's a future where the boundaries between work and personal life continue to blur, challenging traditional notions of the 9-to-5 office job.

Remote work, once considered an exception, has become a viable long-term option for many industries. Companies that embrace remote work will have access to a global talent pool, but they will also need to manage the challenges of maintaining a sense of unity and culture among their dispersed teams. Technology will play a pivotal role in this endeavor, facilitating communication, collaboration, and the tracking of productivity.

Automation and artificial intelligence are transforming the workplace, with many tasks that were previously done by humans being automated. Employees will need to develop skills that complement, rather than compete with, these technologies. The ability to harness the power of AI and automation to enhance productivity and decision-making will be a valuable skill in the future.

Flexible scheduling and alternative work arrangements will continue to gain popularity, allowing employees to tailor their work to their lives, rather than the other way around. This shift will place a greater emphasis on results rather than hours worked, fostering a results-driven work culture.

Diversity and inclusion are not just ethical considerations; they are also good for business. Diverse teams bring a wealth of perspectives and ideas, enhancing innovation and problem-solving. Companies that prioritize diversity and inclusion will be better positioned to attract top talent and serve diverse customer bases.

Sustainability is no longer a choice but a necessity. Companies will be expected to integrate sustainable practices into their operations, from reducing carbon emissions to eliminating single-use plastics in the office. The impact of these efforts will extend beyond the workplace, contributing to a more sustainable future for all.

Reskilling and upskilling are essential in a rapidly changing job market. Employees who take the initiative to learn new skills and adapt to changing technologies will remain competitive and valuable to their organizations. Employers will need to invest in training and development programs to ensure their workforce is up to the challenges of the future.

Well-being initiatives are not mere perks but a fundamental aspect of a successful workplace. Mental health and physical well-being programs will be integrated into the fabric of office culture. This focus on well-being is not just about employee satisfaction; it's about productivity, innovation, and long-term success.

Leadership styles will evolve to accommodate the changing dynamics of the modern office. Traditional hierarchical structures may give way to more agile, collaborative models. The leaders of the future will need to be adaptable, empathetic, and capable of fostering a positive workplace culture.

In conclusion, the future of office work is an exciting and dynamic landscape. It offers opportunities for enhanced productivity, creativity, and well-being, but it also presents challenges that require adaptability and ongoing learning. As we navigate this evolving terrain, the strategies discussed in this book will serve as valuable tools for overcoming the challenges of the modern office. By embracing technology, fostering harmonious workplace relationships, mastering time management, prioritizing well-being, and adapting to change, individuals and organizations can thrive in the ever-changing world of work. The future belongs to those who are willing to innovate, learn, and embrace the opportunities that lie ahead.

"Strategies to Overcome Office Challenges" offers a comprehensive exploration of the multifaceted issues encountered in today's dynamic workplace. With a meticulous breakdown of twenty insightful chapters, this book delves into the heart of office challenges, from embracing technology disruptions to fostering harmonious workplace relationships. Readers will gain valuable insights into mastering time management, recognizing and addressing stress and burnout, and promoting mental and physical well-being in the office.

The book further explores the vital role of leadership in overcoming challenges and dives into the specific struggles faced across various office roles, such as sales and marketing, IT and technical support, management, and human resources. It also examines legal and technological challenges, effective communication, innovation, and the future of office work. "Strategies to Overcome Office Challenges" provides practical solutions, fostering a productive and resilient work environment for today's professionals.

ABOUT THE AUTHOR

Mr. C. P. Kumar is a retired Scientist 'G' from National Institute of Hydrology, Roorkee, Uttarakhand, India. He is also a Reiki Healer and Chakra Balancing practitioner (with pendulum dowsing) and offers Emotional Freedom Technique (EFT) to help individuals with emotional issues. Mr. Kumar has authored many books on technical, spiritual, and social topics.

For further details, you may visit his webpage
https://www.angelfire.com/nh/cpkumar/virgo.html

9 798864 633212